E ... D
FOOTBALL

MICHAEL HEATLEY
AND IAN WELCH

DIAL HOUSE
abc

First published 1996

ISBN 0 7110 2465 0

© Ian Allan Ltd 1996

Published by Dial House

an imprint of Ian Allan Ltd, Terminal House
Station Approach, Shepperton, Surrey TW17
Printed by Ian Allan Printing Ltd,
Coombelands House, Coombelands Lane,
Addlestone Surrey KT15 1HY.

Acknowledgements:

Writing: Michael Heatley
Statistics: Ian Welch
Design: Simon Joslin
Consultant editor: Dennis Turner
All photographs Empics, except:
DM Turner Collection: 5, 6 (both), 7, 1_
19, 22 (bottom), 25, 27 (top), 29, 79 (top
82 (left), 87 (above), 91, 92 (centre), 96
Northdown Collection: 2, 22 (top), 38 (
43, 90
Ken Coton: 92 (top)

Front cover photo: Alan Shearer, spearh
England's Euro 96 campaign.

Previous page: David Batty in the thick
action, watched by team-mate Geoff Th
against Argentina in 1991.

Opposite: The programme for the clash
Scotland in 1971 which finished 3-1 to
England.

Above left: Rivals for the keeper's jersey
Clemence and Peter Shilton.

CONTENTS

INTRODUCTION

Picking the England team has become a national pastime, beloved of experts in public bars nationwide since football began. Yet England began their 1996 campaign as host nation for the European Championship with their next manager the subject of heated debate usually reserved for matters on the pitch.

Terry Venables' decision in late 1995 to step down after Euro '96 not only ended the shortest permanent reign of any England boss since 1946, but the controversy surrounding it reflected the country's wish to once again become a leading force in world football. That had not been the case for the past three decades since a World Cup win, also at home.

The press's depiction of Venables, though not yet as cruel as that of his predecessors Graham Taylor and Bobby Robson, underlined the fact that this was one of sport's pressure jobs: any English club boss thinking of applying either now or in the future should study the facts and figures within this book – one World Cup and precious little else – before giving up his day job.

England didn't even have a manager until 1946, when Walter Winterbottom was appointed to the post. When the national side took on Scotland in its first international in 1872, one of the players was the man doing the choosing, though a committee system would soon be in place. And the fact that England enjoyed a 20-match unbeaten run between 1890 and 1896 makes a good case for a meeting of the minds!

The World Cup kicked off in 1930 – but without England. Two further decades would elapse before we decided to compete, and even then a single-goal defeat against the United States saw headlines made for all the wrong reasons. It wasn't all doom and gloom, though: Lawton and Mortensen finished off World Cup holders Italy in 1948 to prove we could live with the best.

The 1950s saw progress but no silverware, and it was not until Ipswich manager Alf Ramsey took the reins in 1963 that England were not only respected but feared as a world footballing force. Since Ramsey relinquished the post in 1974, five other men (plus caretaker Joe Mercer) have tried to make as great a permanent mark – but none,

until Terry Venables in Euro '96, enjoyed the home advantage Ramsey's immortal eleven made pay. We'd come close – a spot-kick or two away in Italia '90 – but not close enough. Yet with football being the unpredictable game it is, even England's fiercest critics would not discount the possibility of a renaissance.

As we prepare to enter a new millennium, English club football has made as much of a mark on the world game as has its national team, outstanding teams like Arsenal, Liverpool, Nottingham Forest having swept the honours board between them over past decades. Who would be selected to bring similar success to England in Venables' stead remained to be seen at presstime. But *abc England Football* tells all they need to know about the state of national football in England for the past century.

Right: Terry Venables, the man with the nation's hopes resting on his shoulders in June 1996.

1: HISTORY OF THE ENGLAND FOOTBALL TEAM

A place in the national team has always been the aim of any sportsman – and for an English-born footballer the chance to pull the white shirt over his head and bear the three lions on his chest will always be the supreme honour the game can offer.

The biggest team prize in the game, of course, is the World Cup – so for the eleven men who made the most of home advantage to beat West Germany in 1966 and claim the Jules Rimet Trophy, the experience was a lifetime highlight. No schoolboy who watched the game on black and white television will forget the heartbreak of Germany's last minute equaliser...the controversy of Geoff Hurst's goal that bounced behind the line...or the now-familiar exclamation of commentator Kenneth Wolstenholme as Hurst made it safe: 'They think it's all over – it is now!'

That wasn't the end of the England team's quest for glory, of course – and three decades after their World Cup win they once again enjoyed home advantage as the European Championship, held in England for the very first time, stood there for the taking.

England's international history goes back to an era that pre-dates both the World Cup and European Championship, and takes in the now-defunct Home Internationals – a tournament that, before fixture congestion and hooliganism precipitated its demise, set the four Home Countries of England, Scotland, Wales and Northern Ireland against each other in what was always a hard-fought series of games.

Players who, in the normal season, would line up together for 42 games or more strained to kick lumps out of each other as national pride came into play. The England-Scotland fixture was inevitably the most keenly contested, and that is why the resumption of this fixture – albeit for one year only, by virtue of the European Championship draw – was so widely welcomed by players, managers and media alike.

The Home Internationals began in season 1883-84 and until its demise in 1984 was world football's oldest international series. But England's first ever international, against Scotland, pre-dates these by a decade, having taken place in Glasgow on 30 November 1872. Wales appeared on the scene in 1880 and Northern Ireland two years later.

It wasn't until the tournament's third season that England could claim a share of the honours with Scotland, who topped the table outright on the first two occasions. England finished top two seasons later, and the hero of the hour was Preston's Fred Dewhurst who scored a hat-trick as England whipped the 'Auld Enemy' in Glasgow. It was perhaps little wonder that Preston would become the League's first winners in 1888-89 with such a marksman on board.

Professionalism was now the dominant force in football, and the national team was quickly to change in character from 'gentlemen' to 'players'. This had an immediate beneficial effect where games against the Scots were concerned, since the Scottish FA for some time refused to consider international-class Scots who had migrated south to the Football League. This 'anti-Anglo' bias would cost them dear, as England remained unbeaten against all opposition between 1890 and 1896.

Football was catching on quickly as the international winter game, and the result was the formation of an international Football Association. The English FA were

Below: Jack Silcock, a fixture of the Manchester United interwar squad with 449 League and FA Cup appearances, won three caps between 1921 and 1923.

JACK SILCOCK

interest in the game at home where capacity crowds at League games were not unexceptional. New arrivals like Tom Finney and Wilf Mannion joined a handful of seasoned players anxious to make up for lost time. The selection panel put their trust in youth for the first postwar international, against Northern Ireland at Windsor Park. This saw no fewer than nine players making their international débuts; Raich Carter (capped while at Sunderland before the war but now with Derby) and Chelsea's Tommy Lawton were the exceptions. Not that this mattered too much, judging by the 7-2 scoreline to the visitors.

Lawton was among the goals as Holland took on England at Huddersfield's Leeds Road ground in 1947. The Dutch scored twice but conceded eight, four to Lawton. Scotland were the opposition for the first

approached to take the lead, in echoes of cricket and the Marylebone Cricket Club – but they failed to respond and Europe went ahead without them. The FA consented to become a member, but were later to pull out temporarily – a course of action that was to cost them a say in how the first World Cups were to be run.

England's first overseas tour in 1908, the year they won the Olympic Championship, seemed only to confirm the 'Little Englanders' outlook, with four wins out of four against Austria (twice, 6-1 and 11-1), Hungary (7-0) and Bohemia (4-0). Foreign tours would not become commonplace until after World War 1, and indeed it would not be until 1929 that England would be defeated on foreign soil – by Spain, who edged a seven-goal thriller. By then, though, England were no longer regarded as masters of the football world.

The 1930s brought some memorable matches – not all, however, for the right reasons as with the 'Battle of Highbury' in 1934. This saw an England team with seven Arsenal players beat World Champions Italy by a 3-2 margin – but not without a good deal of bad feeling. The game in Germany in 1938 will not be remembered solely for its 6-3 winning scoreline, but the infamous Hitler salute they were to give before the game.

The postwar era saw England carry all before them, buoyed by a huge upsurge of

Top: George Harrison, reported to have one of the fiercest shots ever.

Above: The programme for the England v Scotland clash in April 1924.

Right: Goalkeeper Alan Hodgkinson of Sheffield United won his first cap in 1957 against Scotland.

postwar international at Wembley which ended all-square at 1-1, 98,250 witnessing it. England also played for the first time against the Republic of Ireland, shading the game at Dalymont Park by a Tom Finney goal.

Walter Winterbottom, a man with no pedigree in League management but a sound coaching background, had been selected as England's first manager in 1946. This was not the end of the selection committee, however, for he had to argue his case and remembers more than once that members' own club preferences sometimes came into play, while other players were awarded caps for long service. It wasn't necessarily the best way to create a winning team, but for the moment England's fortunes continued to rise.

Buoyed by 1947 victories against Portugal (10-0) and Belgium (5-2), England were keen to pit their wits against the best. And the defeat of Italy in Turin in 1948 by a 4-0 margin appeared as significant as the Battle of Highbury in throwing down a gauntlet to the world. But they were sadly mistaken, as the Republic of Ireland showed the following year when, at Goodison Park, they removed England's proud record of never having lost against 'continental' (ie non-Home Country) opposition.

The Home Internationals and the World Cup came together in 1949-50 (as they would in 1953-54) to make a qualifying group for the Final stages, to be played in Brazil. The clinching victory against Scotland, albeit by a single goal, was hard-won at a Hampden Park packed to capacity with 133,250 partisan fans. Yet England's single-goal defeat in their first ever international against the United States will go down as a low point in their international record. Eleven strikes of the woodwork counted for nothing as Haitian striker Larry Gaetjens removed England's chances of progressing in their first ever World Cup. Middlesbrough's Wilf Mannion was among those unimpressed. 'Bloody ridiculous,' he puffed. 'Can't we play them again tomorrow?'

Sadly they couldn't

and the only Englishman to play a part in the Final was referee George Reader of Southampton. Not even a 'homer' of a referee, however, could have helped England three years later when Hungary came to Wembley and won 6-3. It was an earth-shattering event, even in an historic year which also brought the Coronation, the ascent of Everest, an Ashes win and the Matthews Cup Final. 'Stan the Man' was also present in a white shirt, alongside the likes of Billy Wright, Stan Mortensen, Jimmy Dickinson and future national boss Alf Ramsey.

They were soundly beaten by the mercurial talents of Puskas, Hidegkuti, Kocsis and Bozsik. When England travelled to meet the 'Magnificent Magyars' on home turf, they returned with an even bigger thrashing, this time 7-1. Change was clearly long overdue – and after returning from the 1954 World Cup in Switzerland it was forthcoming.

England had lost in their third game, a quarter-final against holders Uruguay, but 40 players had been used in the previous two seasons' internationals – a direct consequence of the selection panel system. Winterbottom sought and was given a freer hand, now selecting with the 'help' of just two committee members, and results looked up.

A 16-game unbeaten run from 1955-57 steadied the ship, only for the loss of three key Manchester United men – Roger Byrne, Tommy Taylor and Duncan Edwards – in the Munich air crash to cause further turbulence.

The 1958 World Cup saw the first and only Finals in which all four Home Countries would participate, England having brushed aside Denmark and the Republic of Ireland in their qualifying group. Yet it was Brazil who would triumph, becoming the first team to win outside their own continent, and the most successful Englishman would be Sweden manager George Raynor, whose collection of

Above: Gerry Hitchens watches as Johnny Haynes (behind) shoots in the 1962 match against Switzerland.

veterans and exiles made the most of home advantage to face the South Americans in the Final.

England had held Brazil to a goalless draw, the only side Brazil failed to score against, but perished in a play-off against the USSR. Only winless Scotland had failed to acquit themselves honourably. Brazil's talented young team had included the teenage Pelé, and a far-sighted Winterbottom proposed 'a policy of developing a young team that would play together, mature together and be ready within a four-year cycle'. Unfortunately an attempt to start this in 1959 with a team of mostly Under 21s, including Brian Clough, was abandoned at his colleagues' insistence after a defeat to Sweden and it was 'back to the old regime'.

England had romped through a weak group to qualify for Chile 1962, but – despite the presence of such talents as Greaves, Haynes, Moore, Wilson and Bobby Charlton – trailed behind Hungary in their group and lost in the quarters to Brazil, on their way to a second successive win. Talk began of a combined Home Countries team, but the FA's technical sub-committee rejected this out of hand. Instead, it concluded, 'players must dedicate themselves to the task of improving personal performance'. Both issues are themes that have continued to be discussed to this day...

Winterbottom gave way to Alf Ramsey in 1963, his successor having been chosen because of his domestic success with unfashionable Ipswich Town. He won the post over Winterbottom's right-hand man Jimmy Adamson, still a player, because of the Burnley man's lack of experience.

Early omens were poor – two straight losses away to France and at home to Scotland which these days would have resulted in tabloid tantrums – but fortunately everything came good thereafter. Only four of the next 42 games would see England defeated.

The linchpin of the side was Bobby Moore who, in 1963 against Czechoslovakia, proved that if you're good enough you're old enough by captaining England at the age of 22. It was only his second time in the Number 6 shirt he'd wear with distinction until 1973.

Ramsey's – and England's – crowning achievement was of course the 1966 World Cup, for which they automatically qualified as hosts. Six matches in 19 days was all it took, on the face of it – yet this was the result of much careful planning by the meticulous manager. Not to mention a certain amount of off-the-cuff inspiration.

Of his three dozen pre-World Cup games in charge, 24 were won, eight drawn and just four lost – Championship form in club football terms. The Cup-winning defence first played as a unit in April 1965. Then inspiration came in when he dispensed with wide players, preferring instead the midfield industry of Alan Ball. And in replacing the injured Jimmy Greaves, England's most dangerous home-grown striker, with reserve Geoff Hurst, he fashioned a forward pairing with Roger Hunt that kept running through extra time to press home England's claim to the ultimate prize.

Tails still up, the World Champions went on to register their best ever placing, third, in the European Championship. The semi-final was lost by a single, late goal to Yugoslavia in Florence, a game remembered for the historic dismissal of Spurs midfielder Alan Mullery. His retaliation, spotted by the referee, made him the first England player

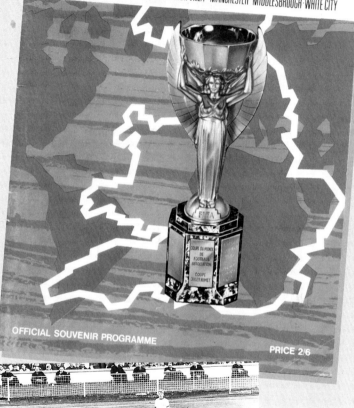

JULES RIMET CUP
WORLD CHAMPIONSHIP
ENGLAND 1966 JULY 11-30

WEMBLEY · EVERTON · SHEFFIELD · SUNDERLAND · ASTON VILLA · MANCHESTER · MIDDLESBROUGH · WHITE CITY

COUPE DU MONDE
DE FOOTBALL
ASSOCIATION

COUPE
JULES RIMET

OFFICIAL SOUVENIR PROGRAMME

PRICE 2/6

Above: The programme for the 1966 World Cup tournament.

Left: World Cup winners Jack Charlton, George Cohen (2) and Bobby Moore stand firm as the West Germans attack in the Final.

ever to be sent off in an international, and a 2-0 win against the USSR was poor consolation for a team that still rightly considered itself the world's best. Indeed, 19 games between that third-place play-off and the next World Cup Finals (for which England, as holders, qualified automatically) would see England lose only once, and that in Brazil.

The World Cup's traditional habit of alternating continents gave Mexico the 1970 tournament – a decision that immediately made England's task of retaining the trophy an uphill struggle. And it wasn't just the rarefied atmosphere that conspired against them: a trumped-up theft charge against skipper Bobby Moore in Colombia during the pre-tournament warm-up unsettled the camp, while keeper Gordon Banks' unavailability through illness for the quarter-final against Germany thrust Chelsea custodian Peter Bonetti into the spotlight.

The outcome of the previous tournament's Final was reversed as England relaxed their grip on the game, a two-goal lead being thrown away. Ramsey (now Sir Alf) had clearly decided to rest midfielders Charlton and Peters' legs for the semi-final and a double substitution ensued: it was the ring-rusty Bonetti, however, who was blamed for two of the three goals that took Germany through. Bobby Charlton, who'd just passed Billy Wright's long-standing 105-cap record, would not represent his country again.

Ramsey's reign was not over despite this setback, and he would lead his team into another European Championship – where once again it was the Germans, now inspired by a new Beckenbauer in Gunter Netzer, who ended their hopes at the quarter-final stage.

In the event, it was England's failure to qualify for the next World Cup that ended an era. And it took place one October 1973 night at Wembley, where Polish goalkeeper Jan Tomaszewski, dubbed a 'clown' by manager turned TV pundit Brian Clough, defied England single (and even, on occasion, double) handedly to secure the all-important draw. Norman Hunter, Bobby Moore's replacement, proved all too fallible, slipping for little Lato to free scorer Domarski.

Ramsey, the World Cup winner, had failed to create a second winning team and paid the penalty. Nevertheless, his was the most successful spell in the England national team's history, with 69 wins and 27 draws from his 113 games and just 17 defeats. Little wonder the FA softened their blow with 'deep appreciation for all Sir Alf has accomplished and the debt owed to him by English football for his loyalty, dedication and integrity'.

Seven-game stopgap Joe Mercer was succeeded by Don Revie, three times Manager of the Year thanks to his achievements with the dour but successful Leeds United. Like Millwall, his team motto at Elland Road might have been 'nobody likes us – we don't care', but this camaraderie was impossible to achieve with players of different clubs who met but rarely. It was an era of constant change: only once in 29 games was the same team fielded twice running. Best performances were reserved for opponents with little significance, though Malcolm Macdonald's five goals against Cyprus in 1975 still represented an outstanding individual performance.

European Championship chances slipped away as eventual winners Czechoslovakia inflicted the first reverse of the Revie reign. The deciding game, a 1-1 draw in Lisbon against Portugal, was received badly by the media due in part to Revie's much-publicised bonus payments for progress – £5,000 a man for the Championship, significant sums for the quarter-finals and beyond. The incentives that might motivate club players made no difference: England were tentative, defensive and lacked class under Revie, and his departure in a cloak of secrecy for a Middle Eastern coaching job in 1977 was not widely mourned.

His replacement was West Ham's Ron Greenwood, a man whose reputation for integrity and attacking football may have swung the powers that be, stung by Revie's defection and uncompromising tactics. He had also, at 55, bowed out of club management but was young enough to meet the challenge of the job.

Greenwood took England to the European Championship Finals in Italy in 1980, though defeat by the host nation consigned them to an early exit. In 1981, he overcame a shock World Cup qualifying defeat against Switzerland – it was later revealed Greenwood quit on the plane home, only to reconsider in the face of 'player power' – to reach the '82 Finals in Spain. *En route*, he masterminded England's first ever victory in the Nep Stadium, belated revenge for Hungary's 1950s humblings, perhaps?

But Kevin Keegan, his captain and most potent attacking force, was troubled by a back injury and, like fellow midfielder Trevor Brooking, unavailable when it mattered: their later introduction against the host nation as substitutes proved insufficient to pull England through, and Greenwood was on his way to well-earned retirement.

Left: Peter Bonetti, thrown in at the deep end as a result of Gordon Banks' illness.

Above: Alf Ramsey took England to the 1966 and 1970 World Cups. He was awarded a knighthood in 1967 and his success has proved impossible for subsequent managers to live up to.

To choose his successor, the FA followed the Ramsey route to Portman Road. Bobby Robson had proved himself at Ipswich with FA Cup, UEFA Cup and two runner's-up positions in the League. Risking the nation's wrath by overlooking Keegan, he saw good away wins against Hungary and Luxembourg nullified by double Wembley blows from Greece (who drew) and Denmark, whose single goal would prove decisive in ruling England out of Euro '84.

He did, however, manage two years later to steer England to the World Finals in Mexico, the scene of Ramsey's downfall in 1970. On the way, his team inflicted a 2-0 defeat on Brazil in their Maracana Stadium, one of the world's best-known hotbeds of football, with Watford's outstanding young flanker John Barnes cementing his place in the national team for years to come with an individual goal that left commentators wondering if one of the home team had slipped the wrong shirt on by accident.

All did not go quite so well in Mexico...initially, at least. The England attack drew blanks against Portugal and Morocco, the latter game seeing the usually unflappable Ray Wilkins dismissed in 100 degree plus heat. But injury forced a change of tactics on Robson and an almost-accidental forging of the Gary Lineker-Peter Beardsley strike partnership that saw the former hit his second international hat-trick. That proved enough to take them to a game against Paraguay and thence to the quarter-finals.

There, the 'hand of God' in the shape of Diego Maradona helped eventual Cup-winners Argentina through by a slim 2-1 margin. Lineker's consolation strike helped him bow out with six goals, a Golden Boot and a lucrative transfer to Barcelona.

The England side then flattered to deceive, qualifying with ease for the 1988 European Championship but losing all three games they played in the German-staged Finals. The Republic of Ireland, Holland, USSR...all triumphed over Robson's boys – and though Eire's single-goal win was bemoaned by the press, due to the presence of World Cup '66 hero Jack Charlton as manager, it should be pointed out the other two sides were the eventual Finalists.

Despite a critical mauling, Robson survived to justify the FA's faith and take England to World Cup 1990 in Italy. Seven games, three with extra time attached, saw them end a barren spell as England made it into the World Cup semi-finals – their best performance since the Wembley win. As in 1966 and 1970, their opponents were West Germany, and this time the teams proved evenly matched.

The tie was decided on penalties – never a satisfactory way of producing a result, and for England a less than effective one. Pearce and Waddle proved unable to convert, and a

Left: The programme the World Cup qualifying match aga Romania in 1981 whic ended goalless.

Below: Wembley Stadium, host to the European Champions Final in June 1996.

Top right: David Platt and Tony Adams rush retrieve the ball durin the match against San Marino in February 19

Bottom right: Graham Taylor feels the weigh of public expectation his shoulders before t November 1993 Worlc Cup qualifying match against San Marino. England went on to w 7-1, having fallen beh to the quickest international goal (nir seconds) ever scored, b still failed to qualify d to previous results.

campaign that had seen wins against Egypt, Belgium and Cameroon and draws with Eire and Holland ended on a low note (they subsequently lost 3-1 in the third-place play-off against Italy).

Striker Gary Lineker, who'd end with 48 goals in 80 internationals, bagged four of these in the competition, while England went home with a trophy – the Fair Play trophy, awarded for incurring the fewest cautions and fouls. Alongside hotshot Lineker, England's shining star of the tournament was Paul Gascoigne, the Newcastle-born midfielder whose tears after incurring a booking that would have ruled him out of Final contention became the image of the campaign.

As with Lineker before, the World Cup proved an effective shop window. Gazza's display won him a lucrative move to Italy, while manager Robson bowed out with dignity – the FA having failed to guarantee his continuing employ – to manage Dutch crack team PSV Eindhoven. He'd take them to the title in his first season, while the man handed the England baton was Aston Villa manager Graham Taylor.

Though Taylor had guided Villa to second place behind Liverpool in 1989-90, his major achievement had been turning Watford into top-flight contenders aided by pop star Elton John's millions. David Platt, his star at Villa who'd been blooded under previous management, became the midfield mainstay

and Sheffield Wednesday's Chris Woods replaced the long-serving Shilton. Few games were won convincingly, but a hard-fought 1-1 draw in Poland took England to the 1992 European Championship Finals.

Held in Sweden, these are now remembered more for Taylor's decision to withdraw captain Gary Lineker in their last match when he stood just one goal short of

Above: Terry Venables and Paul Gascoigne discuss tactics during a training session. The pair linked at Spurs before renewing their link at national level.

Bobby Charlton's record goals tally of 49 and had already announced his decision to retire after the tournament. It was a petty decision that undoubtedly cost Taylor much public sympathy, but in truth England were already as unconvincing as the local police's efforts to curb the hooliganism which had reared its ugly head once more.

Barnes and Stevens had been ruled out by injuries sustained in warm-up matches, and two goalless draws against Denmark and France were followed by a 2-1 defeat against the host nation – this despite a fourth-minute Platt goal. Rebuilding was clearly the order of the day.

Opened with not inconsiderable razzmatazz, the 1994 World Cup Finals in America were designed to launch the round-ball game in the country where, arguably, it had greatest untapped potential. In view of the large number of Irish-American immigrant families, it was as well that the Republic of Ireland qualified – but none of the four Home Countries managed to accompany them to the New World.

The match against Holland that signalled Taylor's demise was one of the more public humiliations a manager had undergone, thanks to a microphone attached to him by a TV documentary team.

The programme that resulted made riveting viewing, and spawned the oft-repeated slogan 'Do I not like that?' but did little for either Taylor or the job he would shortly vacate.

The man selected to replace Taylor was pointedly given the title of coach. Terry Venables had, it was implied, been selected for his ability as a tactician and man-manager likely to bring success to the national team rather than representing a figurehead for English football. Indeed, a 'technical supremo' was to be chosen with wider responsibilities, and Venables had reportedly ruled himself out of contention.

His first dozen games brought steady rather than spectacular progress, but since qualification for the 1996 European Championship was assured as hosts, the forecast was optimistic.

Venables' shock decision to quit after the Finals rather than take England forward to the 1998 World Cup in France was announced six months before the tournament. It represented a blow to the game, and underlined the media pressures that had brought down Graham Taylor before him.

As well as the difficulty of finding a national coach willing to risk his reputation at the hands of the press, the long-term future of the England team is also under threat by pressure groups within FIFA who resent the four Home Countries' separate national identities and believe a Great Britain team would be fairer. There is also the argument, of course, that it would be more successful...but no true England supporter would ever admit to that.

ENGLAND 1996 EUROPEAN CHAMPIONSHIP GAMES

8 June 1996	v	Switzerland
15 June 1996	v	Scotland
18 June 1996	v	Holland
22 June 1996		Quarter-Final
26 June 1996		Semi-Final
30 June 1996		Final

ENGLAND 1998 WORLD CUP QUALIFYING GAMES

1 September 1996	v	Moldova	(A)
9 October 1996	v	Poland	(H)
9 November 1996	v	Georgia	(A)
23 February 1997	v	Italy	(H)
30 April 1997	v	Georgia	(H)
31 May 1997	v	Poland	(A)
10 September 1997	v	Moldova	(H)
11 October 1997	v	Italy	(A)

International match-by-match results from 1872-1995 (plus ten great games)

YEAR	DATE	MATCH	VENUE	SCORE			
1872	30 November	F	Glasgow	England	0	Scotland	0
1873	8 March	F	Kennington Oval	England	4	Scotland	2
1874	7 March	F	Glasgow	England	1	Scotland	2
1875	6 March	F	Kennington Oval	England	2	Scotland	2
1876	4 March	F	Glasgow	England	0	Scotland	3
1877	3 March	F	Kennington Oval	England	1	Scotland	3
1878	2 March	F	Glasgow	England	2	Scotland	7
1879	18 January	F	Kennington Oval	England	2	Wales	1
	5 April	F	Kennington Oval	England	5	Scotland	4
1880	13 March	F	Glasgow	England	4	Scotland	5
	15 March	F	Wrexham	England	3	Wales	2
1881	26 February	F	Blackburn	England	0	Wales	1
	12 March	F	Kennington Oval	England	1	Scotland	6
1882	18 February	F	Belfast	England	13	Ireland	0
	11 March	F	Glasgow	England	1	Scotland	5
	13 March	F	Wrexham	England	3	Wales	5
1883	3 February	HC	Kennington Oval	England	5	Wales	0
	24 February	HC	Liverpool	England	7	Ireland	0
	10 March	HC	Sheffield	England	2	Scotland	3
1884	23 February	HC	Belfast	England	8	Ireland	1
	15 March	HC	Glasgow	England	0	Scotland	1
	17 March	HC	Wrexham	England	4	Wales	0
1885	28 February	HC	Manchester	England	4	Ireland	0
	14 March	HC	Blackburn	England	1	Wales	1
	21 March	HC	Kennington Oval	England	1	Scotland	1
1886	13 March	HC	Belfast	England	6	Ireland	1
	29 March	HC	Wrexham	England	3	Wales	1
	31 March	HC	Glasgow	England	1	Scotland	1
1887	5 February	HC	Sheffield	England	7	Ireland	0
	26 February	HC	Kennington Oval	England	4	Wales	0
	19 March	HC	Blackburn	England	2	Scotland	3
1888	4 February	HC	Crewe	England	5	Wales	1
	17 March	HC	Glasgow	England	5	Scotland	0
	31 March	HC	Belfast	England	5	Ireland	1
1889	23 February	HC	Stoke-on-Trent	England	4	Wales	1
	2 March	HC	Everton	England	6	Ireland	1
	13 April	HC	Kennington Oval	England	2	Scotland	3
1890	15 March•	HC	Belfast	England	9	Ireland	1
	15 March•	HC	Wrexham	England	3	Wales	1
	5 April	HC	Glasgow	England	1	Scotland	1
1891	7 March•	HC	Sunderland	England	4	Wales	1
	7 March•	HC	Wolverhampton	England	6	Ireland	1
	6 April	HC	Blackburn	England	2	Scotland	1
1892	5 March•	HC	Wrexham	England	2	Wales	0
	5 March•	HC	Belfast	England	2	Ireland	0
	2 April	HC	Glasgow	England	4	Scotland	1
1893	25 February	HC	Birmingham	England	6	Ireland	1
	13 March	HC	Stoke-on-Trent	England	6	Wales	0
	1 April	HC	Richmond	England	5	Scotland	2
1894	3 March	HC	Belfast	England	2	Ireland	2

7 DECEMBER 1932

England	4
Austria	3
Venue: Stamford Bridge	

Two decades before Hungary came to Wembley and taught England an unforgettable lesson, Austria sent their so-called *Wunderteam* to London hoping to be the first foreign team to overturn the self-styled fathers of football on their home turf. Spain, who had beaten England 3-2 in 1929, came to Highbury two years later and lost 7-1, so if nothing else, England were a formidable force with their crowd behind them.

Hampson's early opening goal, then, was the cue for Austria to roll over – but though he made it two after 26 minutes, the Austrians had regained their composure. Vogl missed an empty net just before half-time when a goal might have proved psychologically vital, but right-winger Zischek reduced the arrears after 51 minutes. Red-shirted Austria buzzed with a new confidence, and it was much against the run of play when Houghton's free-kick rebounded off the Austrian wall to give the hosts a 3-1 advantage.

Centre-forward Sindelar converted some sustained pressure to bring the score to 3-2, but an outstanding long-range drive from Derby winger Crooks again gave England a flattering margin. Austria finally got the rub of the green when Zischek scored his second after obstruction at a corner-kick, but the end result was the expected home win. What had not been anticipated was Austria's superb passing game: had they been able to convert their chances as well, the events of 1953 might not have been as historic.

England: Hibbs, Goodall, Blenkinsop, Strange, Hart, Keen, Crooks, Jack, Hampson, Walker, Houghton.

Right: Bolton and Arsenal's interwar star inside-right David Jack won nine caps (three goals) following his 1924 début against Scotland. He did not appear on the scoresheet in this, his last England game.

YEAR	DATE	MATCH	VENUE	SCORE			
1894	12 March	HC	Wrexham	England	5	Wales	1
	7 April	HC	Glasgow	England	2	Scotland	2
1895	9 March	HC	Derby	England	9	Ireland	0
	18 March	HC	Queen's Club, Kensington	England	1	Wales	1
	6 April	HC	Everton	England	3	Scotland	0
1896	7 March	HC	Belfast	England	2	Ireland	0
	16 March	HC	Cardiff	England	9	Wales	1
	4 April	HC	Glasgow	England	1	Scotland	2
1897	20 February	HC	Nottingham	England	6	Ireland	0
	29 March	HC	Sheffield	England	4	Wales	0
	3 April	HC	Crystal Palace	England	1	Scotland	2
1898	5 March	HC	Belfast	England	3	Ireland	2
	28 March	HC	Wrexham	England	3	Wales	0
	2 April	HC	Glasgow	England	3	Scotland	1
1899	18 February	HC	Sunderland	England	13	Ireland	2
	20 March	HC	Bristol	England	4	Wales	1
	8 April	HC	Birmingham	England	2	Scotland	1
1900	17 March	HC	Dublin	England	2	Ireland	0
	26 March	HC	Cardiff	England	1	Wales	1
	7 April	HC	Glasgow	England	1	Scotland	4
1901	9 March	HC	Southampton	England	3	Ireland	0

YEAR	DATE	MATCH	VENUE		SCORE			
1901	18 March	HC	Newcastle	England	6	Wales	0
	30 March	HC	Crystal Palace	England	2	Scotland	2
1902	3 March	HC	Wrexham	England	0	Wales	0
	22 March	HC	Beflast	England	1	Ireland	0
	5 April	HC	Glasgow	England	1	Scotland	1
	Match abandoned following the collapse of a stand						
	3 May	HC	Birmingham	England	2	Scotland	2
1903	14 February	HC	Wolverhampton	England	4	Ireland	0
	2 March	HC	Portsmouth	England	2	Wales	1
	4 April	HC	Sheffield	England	1	Scotland	2
1904	29 February	HC	Wrexham	England	2	Wales	2
	12 March	HC	Belfast	England	3	Ireland	1
	9 April	HC	Glasgow	England	1	Scotland	0
1905	25 February	HC	Middlesbrough	England	1	Ireland	1
	27 March	HC	Liverpool	England	3	Wales	1
	1 April	HC	Crystal Palace	England	1	Scotland	0
1906	17 February	HC	Belfast	England	5	Ireland	0
	19 March	HC	Cardiff	England	1	Wales	0
	7 April	HC	Glasgow	England	1	Scotland	2
1907	16 February	HC	Everton	England	1	Ireland	0

14 NOVEMBER 1934

England	3
Italy	2
Venue: Highbury	

This fixture was billed as Arsenal v Italy, due to the unprecedented presence of seven players from the north London club in a game played at their home ground. It entered football folklore as the 'Battle of Highbury' as the current World Champions lost both the game and their cool.

England hadn't entered the World Cup, so had a point to prove – but in the second minute visiting centre-half Monti broke a bone in his foot after an accidental clash with Ted Drake. Down to ten men and with substitutes still unheard-of, Italy set about exacting revenge, but were three down at the

break through Brook (2) and Drake. The Manchester City winger could have had a hat-trick, but keeper Ceresoli was equal to his penalty.

The Italians, who would go on to retain the World Cup four years later, came out to play football in the second half, and the approach nearly paid off. Inter Milan's Giuseppe Meazza, the man who would hold the trophy aloft in France, scored twice in memorable style to set up a closer finish than could have been expected.

Eddie Hapgood, however, would remember his first occasion of captaining his country for the broken nose he picked up in the 'Battle of Highbury'.
England: Moss, Male, Hapgood, Britton, Barker, Copping, Matthews, Bowden, Drake, Bastin, Brook.

Left: Left-half Wilf Copping attacks the Italians' goal during the 1934 'Battle of Highbury'. The former miner, who signed for Arsenal in March, was joined in the team by six fellow Gunners.

YEAR	DATE	MATCH	VENUE	SCORE			
1907	18 March	HC	Fulham	England	1	Wales	1
	6 April	HC	Newcastle	England	1	Scotland	1
1908	15 February	HC	Belfast	England	3	Ireland	1
	16 March	HC	Wrexham	England	7	Wales	1
	4 April	HC	Glasgow	England	1	Scotland	1
	6 June	F	Vienna	England	6	Austria	1
	8 June	F	Vienna	England	11	Austria	1
	10 June	F	Budapest	England	7	Hungary	0
	13 June	F	Prague	England	4	Bohemia	0
1909	13 February	HC	Bradford	England	4	Ireland	0
	15 March	HC	Nottingham	England	2	Wales	0
	3 April	HC	Crystal Palace	England	2	Scotland	0
	29 May	F	Budapest	England	4	Hungary	2
	31 May	F	Budapest	England	8	Hungary	2
	1 June	F	Vienna	England	8	Austria	1
1910	12 February	HC	Belfast	England	1	Ireland	1
	14 March	HC	Cardiff	England	1	Wales	0
	2 April	HC	Glasgow	England	0	Scotland	2
1911	11 February	HC	Derby	England	2	Ireland	1
	13 March	HC	Millwall	England	3	Wales	0
	1 April	HC	Everton	England	1	Scotland	1
1912	10 February	HC	Dublin	England	6	Ireland	1
	11 March	HC	Wrexham	England	2	Wales	0
	23 March	HC	Glasgow	England	1	Scotland	1
1913	15 February	HC	Belfast	England	1	Ireland	2
	17 March	HC	Bristol	England	4	Wales	3
	5 April	HC	Stamford Bridge	England	1	Scotland	0
1914	14 February	HC	Middlesbrough	England	0	Ireland	3
	16 March	HC	Cardiff	England	2	Wales	0
	4 April	HC	Glasgow	England	1	Scotland	3
1919	25 October	HC	Belfast	England	1	Ireland	1
1920	15 March	HC	Highbury	England	1	Wales	2
	10 April	HC	Sheffield	England	5	Scotland	4
	23 October	HC	Sunderland	England	2	Ireland	0
1921	14 March	HC	Cardiff	England	0	Wales	0
	9 April	HC	Glasgow	England	0	Scotland	3
	21 May	F	Brussels	England	2	Belgium	0
	22 October	HC	Belfast	England	1	N Ireland	1
1922	13 March	HC	Liverpool	England	1	Wales	0
	8 April	HC	Villa Park	England	0	Scotland	1
	21 October	HC	West Bromwich	England	2	N Ireland	0
1923	5 March	HC	Cardiff	England	2	Wales	2
	19 March	F	Highbury	England	6	Belgium	1
	14 April	HC	Glasgow	England	2	Scotland	2
	10 May	F	Paris	England	4	France	1
	21 May	F	Stockholm	England	4	Sweden	2
	24 May	F	Stockholm	England	3	Sweden	1
	20 October	HC	Belfast	England	1	N Ireland	2
	1 November	F	Antwerp	England	2	Belgium	2
1924	3 March	HC	Blackburn	England	1	Wales	2
	12 April	HC	Wembley	England	1	Scotland	1
	17 May	F	Paris	England	3	France	1
	22 October	HC	Everton	England	3	N Ireland	1
	8 December	F	West Bromwich	England	4	Belgium	0
1925	28 February	HC	Swansea	England	2	Wales	1

14 MAY 1938	
England	6
Germany	3
Venue: Berlin	

England ventured to the Olympic Stadium in Berlin in 1938 aware that national pride was at stake. 'All sensed that this was not merely a football match but something deeper,' captain Eddie Hapgood would later recall. 'It was a challenge from Germany which England had to answer. And not only to answer, but to defeat.'

The Arsenal left-back, one of five capital-based players in the team, was at least a seasoned international: Sheffield Wednesday inside-right Jackie Robinson was making his début at just 19.

All were obliged to give the Hitler salute which according to Cliff Bastin caused 'much muttering in the ranks'. FA secretary Stanley Rous responded that 'the row really started later'...but whatever the truth, England answered the Germans where it counted – on the pitch – with an unprecedented will to win.

They were 4-1 up at half-time, début boy Robinson notching the second after Germany had equalised Bastin's opening volley. Broom and Matthews had established a comfortable margin, and though both sides notched twice more in the second period, Robinson and Goulden England's scorers, the game had effectively been won. The German team had been unable to match their vociferous supporters' expectations, and England had taken advantage in what was to be one of their last dozen peacetime internationals.

England: Woodley, Sproston, Hapgood, Willingham, Young, Welsh, Matthews, Robinson, Broome, Goulden, Bastin.

Left: England outside-left Cliff Bastin had won all the domestic trophies the game had to offer by the age of 19. He would gain just 21 caps as World War 2 denied him in his prime.

C. BASTIN

YEAR	DATE	MATCH	VENUE	SCORE			
1925	4 April	HC	Glasgow	England	0	Scotland	2
	21 May	F	Paris	England	3	France	2
	24 October	HC	Belfast	England	0	N Ireland	0
1926	1 March	HC	Crystal Palace	England	1	Wales	3
	17 April	HC	Manchester	England	1	Scotland	0
	24 May	F	Antwerp	England	5	Belgium	3
	20 October	HC	Liverpool	England	3	N Ireland	3
1927	12 February	HC	Wrexham	England	3	Wales	3
	2 April	HC	Glasgow	England	2	Scotland	1
	11 May	F	Brussels	England	9	Belgium	1
	21 May	F	Luxembourg	England	5	Luxembourg	2
	26 May	F	Paris	England	6	France	0
	22 October	HC	Belfast	England	0	N Ireland	2
	28 November	HC	Burnley	England	1	Wales	2
1928	31 March	HC	Wembley	England	1	Scotland	5
	17 May	F	Paris	England	5	France	1
	19 May	F	Antwerp	England	3	Belgium	1
	22 October	HC	Everton	England	2	N Ireland	1
	17 November	HC	Swansea	England	3	Wales	2
1929	13 April	HC	Glasgow	England	0	Scotland	1
	9 May	F	Paris	England	4	France	1
	11 May	F	Brussels	England	5	Belgium	1
	15 May	F	Madrid	England	3	Spain	4
	19 October	HC	Belfast	England	3	N Ireland	0
	20 November	HC	Stamford Bridge	England	6	Wales	0
1930	5 April	HC	Wembley	England	5	Scotland	2
	10 May	F	Berlin	England	3	Germany	3
	14 May	F	Vienna	England	0	Austria	0
	20 October	HC	Sheffield	England	5	N Ireland	1
	22 November	HC	Wrexham	England	4	Wales	0
1931	28 March	HC	Glasgow	England	0	Scotland	2
	14 May	F	Paris	England	2	France	5
	16 May	F	Brussels	England	4	Belgium	1
	17 October	HC	Belfast	England	6	N Ireland	2
	18 November	HC	Liverpool	England	3	Wales	1
	9 December	F	Highbury	England	7	Spain	1
1932	9 April	HC	Wembley	England	3	Scotland	0
	17 October	HC	Blackpool	England	1	N Ireland	0
	16 November	HC	Wrexham	England	0	Wales	0
	7 December	F	Stamford Bridge	England	4	Austria	3
1933	1 April	HC	Glasgow	England	1	Scotland	2
	13 May	F	Rome	England	1	Italy	1
	20 May	F	Berne	England	4	Switzerland	0
	14 October	HC	Belfast	England	3	N Ireland	0
	15 November	HC	Newcastle	England	1	Wales	2
	6 December	F	Tottenham	England	4	France	1
1934	14 April	HC	Wembley	England	3	Scotland	0
	10 May	F	Budapest	England	1	Hungary	2
	16 May	F	Prague	England	1	Czechoslovakia	2
	29 September	HC	Cardiff	England	4	Wales	0
	14 November	F	Highbury	England	3	Italy	2
1935	6 February	HC	Everton	England	2	N Ireland	1
	6 April	HC	Glasgow	England	0	Scotland	2
	18 May	F	Amsterdam	England	1	Holland	0
	19 October	HC	Belfast	England	3	N Ireland	1

YEAR	DATE	MATCH	VENUE	SCORE			
1935	4 December	F	Tottenham	England	3	Germany	0
1936	5 February	HC	Wolverhampton	England	1	Wales	2
	4 April	HC	Wembley	England	1	Scotland	1
	6 May	F	Vienna	England	1	Austria	2
	9 May	F	Brussels	England	2	Belgium	3
	17 October	HC	Cardiff	England	1	Wales	2
	18 November	HC	Stoke-on-Trent	England	3	N Ireland	1
	2 December	F	Highbury	England	6	Hungary	2
1937	17 April	HC	Glasgow	England	1	Scotland	3
	14 May	F	Oslo	England	6	Norway	0
	17 May	F	Stockholm	England	4	Sweden	0
	20 May	F	Helsinki	England	8	Finland	0
	23 October	HC	Belfast	England	5	N Ireland	1
	17 November	HC	Middlesbrough	England	2	Wales	1
	1 December	F	Tottenham	England	5	Czechoslovakia	4
1938	9 April	HC	Wembley	England	0	Scotland	1
	14 May	F	Berlin	England	6	Germany	3
	21 May	F	Zurich	England	1	Switzerland	2
	26 May	F	Paris	England	4	France	2
	22 October	HC	Cardiff	England	2	Wales	4
	26 October	F	Highbury	England	3	FIFA	0
	9 November	F	Newcastle	England	4	Norway	0
	16 November	HC	Manchester	England	7	N Ireland	0
1939	15 April	HC	Glasgow	England	2	Scotland	1
	13 May	F	Milan	England	2	Italy	1
	18 May	F	Belgrade	England	1	Yugoslavia	2
	24 May	F	Bucharest	England	2	Romania	0
1946	28 September	HC	Belfast	England	7	N Ireland	2
	30 September	F	Dublin	England	1	Eire	0
	13 November	HC	Manchester	England	3	Wales	0

16 MAY 1948

England	4
Italy	0
Venue: Turin	

Maybe it was the euphoria of winning the war, just three years earlier – but England emerged in peacetime's 'Golden Age' determined to prove themselves a world force in football.

With a 10-0 win against Portugal under their belts, they prepared to measure themselves against the Italians – and instead of heading for Turin with a defensive formation, looking to sneak a counter-attack, the same forward line was played.

England had two world-class right-wingers in Stan Matthews and Tom Finney, so the decision was made to play Finney on the left, offering a double-sided feed to strikers Mortensen and Lawton.

That Italy's team was based around the great Torino club side that was cruelly to perish in a plane crash the following year

made a four-goal victory margin even more impressive than the Portuguese massacre. Mortensen and Lawton notched before the interval, the former with a cross shot that deceived keeper Bacigalupo, but Manchester City's Frank Swift, England's first ever goalkeeping captain, was called upon to perform heroically at the other end to prevent a reply.

Twice in the second half Matthews and Wilf Mannion combined to set up Finney, who completed a handsome victory. Italy were in no way four goals inferior, but the game showed England's determination to shine in the postwar football world.

Sadly, their first World Cup campaign was not to end as gloriously two years later and it is a replay of this clash – in October 1997 – that many believe will decide who finishes top of England's 1998 World Cup qualifying group.

England: Swift, Scott, Howe, Wright, Franklin, Cockburn, Matthews, Mortensen, Lawton, Mannion, Finney.

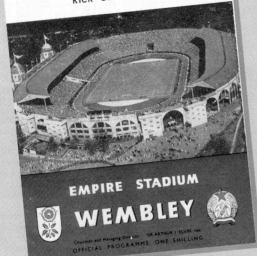

Above: Inside-left Jackie Sewell of Sheffield Wednesday scores England's first goal against the Hungarians at Wembley.

Left: The match programme.

25 NOVEMBER 1953

England	3
Hungary	6
Venue: Wembley	

It's rare that a defeat turns out to be a blessing in disguise, but Hungary's dazzling demolition of England at their newly-confirmed national home of Wembley put into perspective ambitions of ruling the world game. It was officially a friendly but no one – least of all legends like Wright, Matthews and Ramsey – would forget England's first ever home defeat by a foreign side (bar the Republic of Ireland's 2-0 win at Goodison in 1949).

The Hungarians had suffered postwar exile as an Iron Curtain country, but had resumed under coach Gyula Mandi to win the 1952 Olympic tournament – and with 'Galloping Major' Ferenc Puskas pulling the on-field strings from midfield, they tore England apart.

Deep-lying centre-forward Nandor Hidegkuti baffled England's defence: his hat-trick included a 20-yarder in the first minute that speared past astonished keeper Gil Merrick, while Puskas, who scored 85 times in 84 internationals, more than maintained his goal-a-game average with a brace that included one which saw England captain Billy Wright, in the words of one distinguished writer, 'like a fire engine arriving too late for the wrong blaze'.

Right-half Bozsic hit a cracker from outside the area to complete the rout – and though Alf Ramsey would use this to motivate his construction of a World Cup-winning team, they never emulated the Magnificent Magyars' style.

England: Merrick, Ramsey, Eckersley, Wright, Johnston, Dickinson, Matthews, Taylor, Mortensen, Sewell, Robb.

YEAR	DATE	MATCH	VENUE	SCORE			
1946	27 November	F	Huddersfield	England	8	Holland	2
1947	12 April	HC	Wembley	England	1	Scotland	1
	3 May	F	Highbury	England	3	France	0
	18 May	F	Zurich	England	0	Switzerland	1
	25 May	F	Lisbon	England	10	Portugal	0
	21 September	F	Brussels	England	5	Belgium	2
	18 October	HC	Cardiff	England	3	Wales	0
	5 November	HC	Everton	England	2	N Ireland	2
	19 November	F	Highbury	England	4	Sweden	2
1948	10 April	HC	Glasgow	England	2	Scotland	0
	16 May	F	Turin	England	4	Italy	0
	26 September	F	Copenhagen	England	0	Denmark	0
	9 October	HC	Belfast	England	6	N Ireland	2
	10 November	HC	Birmingham	England	1	Wales	0
	2 December	F	Highbury	England	6	Switzerland	0
1949	9 April	HC	Wembley	England	1	Scotland	3
	13 May	F	Stockholm	England	1	Sweden	3
	18 May	F	Oslo	England	4	Norway	1
	22 May	F	Paris	England	3	France	1
	21 September	F	Everton	England	0	Eire	2
	15 October	HC/WCQ	Cardiff	England	4	Wales	1
	16 November	HC/WCQ	Manchester	England	9	N Ireland	2
	30 November	F	Tottenham	England	2	Italy	0
1950	15 April	HC/WCQ	Glasgow	England	1	Scotland	0
	14 May	F	Lisbon	England	5	Portugal	3
	18 May	F	Brussels	England	4	Belgium	1
	25 June	WC	Rio de Janeiro	England	2	Chile	0
	29 June	WC	Belo Horizonte	England	0	USA	1
	2 July	WC	Rio de Janeiro	England	0	Spain	1
	7 October	HC	Belfast	England	4	N Ireland	1
	15 November	HC	Sunderland	England	4	Wales	2
	22 November	F	Highbury	England	2	Yugoslavia	2

YEAR	DATE	MATCH	VENUE	SCORE			
1951	14 April	HC	Wembley	England	2	Scotland	3
	9 May	F	Wembley	England	2	Argentina	1
	19 May	F	Everton	England	5	Portugal	2
	3 October	F	Highbury	England	2	France	2
	20 October	HC	Cardiff	England	1	Wales	1
	14 November	HC	Birmingham	England	2	N Ireland	0
	28 November	F	Wembley	England	2	Austria	2
1952	5 April	HC	Glasgow	England	2	Scotland	1
	18 May	F	Florence	England	1	Italy	1
	25 May	F	Vienna	England	3	Austria	2
	28 May	F	Zurich	England	3	Switzerland	0
	4 October	HC	Belfast	England	2	N Ireland	2
	12 November	HC	Wembley	England	5	Wales	2
	26 November	F	Wembley	England	5	Belgium	0
1953	18 April	HC	Wembley	England	2	Scotland	2
	17 May	F	Buenos Aires	England	0	Argentina	0
	Abandoned after 20 minutes due to torrential rain						
	24 May	F	Santiago	England	2	Chile	1
	31 May	F	Montevideo	England	1	Uruguay	2
	8 June	F	New York	England	6	USA	3
	10 October	HC/WCQ	Cardiff	England	4	Wales	1
	21 October	F	Wembley	England	4	Rest of Europe	4
	11 November	HC/WCQ	Liverpool	England	3	N Ireland	1
	25 November	F	Wembley	England	3	Hungary	6
1954	3 April	HC/WCQ	Glasgow	England	4	Scotland	2
	16 May	F	Belgrade	England	0	Yugoslavia	1
	23 May	F	Budapest	England	1	Hungary	7
	17 June	WC	Basle	England	4	Belgium	4
	20 June	WC	Berne	England	2	Switzerland	0
	26 June	WC	Basle	England	2	Uruguay	4
	2 October	HC	Belfast	England	2	N Ireland	0
	10 November	HC	Wembley	England	3	Wales	2
	1 December	F	Wembley	England	3	W Germany	1
1955	2 April	HC	Wembley	England	7	Scotland	2
	15 May	F	Paris	England	0	France	1
	18 May	F	Madrid	England	1	Spain	1
	22 May	F	Oporto	England	1	Portugal	3
	2 October	F	Copenhagen	England	5	Denmark	1
	22 October	HC	Cardiff	England	1	Wales	2
	2 November	HC	Wembley	England	3	N Ireland	0
	30 November	F	Wembley	England	4	Spain	1
1956	14 April	HC	Glasgow	England	1	Scotland	1
	9 May	F	Wembley	England	4	Brazil	2
	16 May	F	Stockholm	England	0	Sweden	1
	20 May	F	Helsinki	England	5	Finland	1
	26 May	F	Berlin	England	3	W Germany	1
	6 October	HC	Belfast	England	1	N Ireland	1
	14 November	HC	Wembley	England	3	Wales	1
	28 November	F	Wembley	England	3	Yugoslavia	0
	5 December	WCQ	Wolverhampton	England	5	Denmark	2
1957	6 April	HC	Wembley	England	2	Scotland	1
	8 May	WCQ	Wembley	England	5	Eire	1
	15 May	WCQ	Copenhagen	England	4	Denmark	1
	19 May	WCQ	Dublin	England	1	Eire	1
	19 October	HC	Cardiff	England	4	Wales	0
	6 November	HC	Wembley	England	2	N Ireland	3

15 APRIL 1961	
England	9
Scotland	3
Venue: Wembley	

'What's the time? Nine past Haffey!' read the joke on one back page after England's record win over their nearest and most bitter rivals. This was the showpiece of the Home Internationals, and injury-hit Scotland's use of 22 players in the three fixtures against England, Wales and Northern Ireland reflected their disarray.

The killer goal was the fourth from Bryan Douglas that gave England a two-goal cushion. Jimmy Greaves, renowned for his goal-poaching, had taken a quick free-kick to release the Blackburn player, allegedly from the wrong spot – but Scotland's heads went down when their protests went unheeded. Greaves (3), Smith (2), Haynes (2) and Robson completed the rout, with Mackay, Wilson and Quinn responding for the dejected visitors.

Celtic keeper Frank Haffey, third choice before Scotland's injury crisis struck, was the most dejected man on the pitch, but a square back line had let Greaves and his fellow forwards plunder at will.

Though national manager Walter Winterbottom must have walked away from Wembley with a spring in his step, this would not prove a foretaste of success in World Cup '62. And though Bobby Robson and Johnny Haynes were the playmakers who made this victory possible, only one of England's XI here, Bobby Charlton, would grace Wembley as a winner in 1966.

England: Springett, Armfield, McNeil, Robson, Swan, Flowers, Douglas, Greaves, Smith, Haynes, Charlton.

Below: The following year's England team contained eight of Scotland's tormentors.
Back row, left to right: Armfield, Robson, Swan, Springett, Flowers, Wilson.
Front row: Connelly, Douglas, Pointer, Haynes, Charlton.

30 JULY 1966

England	4
West Germany	2
Venue: Wembley	

The fairytale story had a fairytale ending when England took the World Cup in front of their own fans. Wearing an unfamiliar change strip of red, Alf Ramsey's eleven became only the third hosts (after Uruguay in 1930 and Italy in 1934) to make home advantage count.

The visitors went ahead after 13 minutes through Helmut Haller, Geoff Hurst justifying his selection over Jimmy Greaves six minutes later when nodding in a free-kick from club-mate Bobby Moore. The two well-matched teams then locked horns until the 78th minute when Martin Peters, dubbed 'ten years ahead of his time' by Alf Ramsey and another West Ham stalwart, ghosted in to pick up a rebound.

Wolfgang Weber's last-gasp equaliser stemmed from a disputed free-kick – but there was no time for dissent as an extra half-hour loomed. And it was England who edged ahead, again from a controversial incident when Geoff Hurst's shot bounced down from the bar and, according to the Russian linesman, across the line.

With German heads down, Hurst's fourth was a formality. The crowds were already spilling onto the pitch as his drive beat keeper Sepp Maier, inspiring celebrations countrywide.

It was English football's greatest moment and one which has never been eclipsed. Even though Germany exacted revenge at Mexico '70, the Jules Rimet trophy held aloft by Bobby Moore remains a potent image for all fans of the national game.

England: Banks, Cohen, Wilson, Stiles, J Charlton, Moore, Ball, Hurst, Hunt, R Charlton, Peters.

YEAR	DATE	MATCH	VENUE	SCORE			
1957	27 November	F	Wembley	England	4	France	0
1958	19 April	HC	Glasgow	England	4	Scotland	0
	7 May	F	Wembley	England	2	Portugal	1
	11 May	F	Belgrade	England	0	Yugoslavia	5
	18 May	F	Moscow	England	1	USSR	1
	6 June	WC	Gothenburg	England	2	USSR	2
	11 June	WC	Gothenburg	England	0	Brazil	0
	15 June	WC	Boras	England	2	Austria	2
	17 June	WC	Gothenburg	England	0	USSR	1
	4 October	HC	Belfast	England	3	N Ireland	3
	22 October	F	Wembley	England	5	USSR	0
	26 November	HC	Birmingham	England	2	Wales	2
1959	11 April	HC	Wembley	England	1	Scotland	0
	6 May	F	Wembley	England	2	Italy	2
	13 May	F	Rio de Janeiro	England	0	Brazil	2
	17 May	F	Lima	England	1	Peru	4
	24 May	F	Mexico City	England	1	Mexico	2
	28 May	F	Los Angeles	England	8	USA	1
	17 October	HC	Cardiff	England	1	Wales	1
	28 October	F	Wembley	England	2	Sweden	3
	18 November	HC	Wembley	England	2	N Ireland	1
1960	9 April	HC	Glasgow	England	1	Scotland	1
	11 May	F	Wembley	England	3	Yugoslavia	3
	15 May	F	Madrid	England	0	Spain	3
	22 May	F	Budapest	England	0	Hungary	2
	8 October	HC	Belfast	England	5	N Ireland	2
	19 October	WCQ	Luxembourg	England	9	Luxembourg	0
	26 October	F	Wembley	England	4	Spain	2
	23 November	HC	Wembley	England	5	Wales	1
1961	15 April	HC	Wembley	England	9	Scotland	3
	10 May	F	Wembley	England	8	Mexico	0
	21 May	WCQ	Lisbon	England	1	Portugal	1

WORLD CHAMPIONSHIP
JULES RIMET CUP

Final

ENGLAND v WEST GERMANY
SATURDAY · JULY 30 · 1966
EMPIRE STADIUM
WEMBLEY

SOUVENIR
PROGRAMME

PRICE
2/6

Above: The programme for the 1966 World Cup Final, watched by 100,000 at Wembley and TV millions worldwide.

Left: Captain Bobby Moore holds the coveted trophy aloft.

YEAR	DATE	MATCH	VENUE	SCORE			
1961	24 May	F	Rome	England	3	Italy	2
	27 May	F	Vienna	England	1	Austria	3
	28 September	WCQ	Highbury	England	4	Luxembourg	1
	14 October	HC	Cardiff	England	1	Wales	1
	25 October	WCQ	Wembley	England	2	Portugal	0
	22 November	HC	Wembley	England	1	N Ireland	1
1962	4 April	F	Wembley	England	3	Austria	1
	14 April	HC	Glasgow	England	0	Scotland	2
	9 May	F	Wembley	England	3	Switzerland	1
	20 May	F	Lima	England	4	Peru	0
	31 May	WC	Rancagua	England	1	Hungary	2
	2 June	WC	Rancagua	England	3	Argentina	1
	7 June	WC	Rancagua	England	0	Bulgaria	0
	10 June	WC	Vina del Mar	England	1	Brazil	3
	3 October	ENC	Sheffield	England	1	France	1
	20 October	HC	Belfast	England	3	N Ireland	1
	21 November	HC	Wembley	England	4	Wales	0
1963	27 February	ENC	Paris	England	2	France	5
	6 April	HC	Wembley	England	1	Scotland	2
	8 May	F	Wembley	England	1	Brazil	1
	29 May	F	Bratislava	England	4	Czechoslovakia	2
	2 June	F	Leipzig	England	2	E Germany	1
	5 June	F	Basle	England	8	Switzerland	1
	12 October	HC	Cardiff	England	4	Wales	0
	23 October	F	Wembley	England	2	Rest of World	1
	20 November	HC	Wembley	England	8	N Ireland	3
1964	11 April	HC	Glasgow	England	0	Scotland	1
	6 May	F	Wembley	England	2	Uruguay	1
	17 May	F	Lisbon	England	4	Portugal	3
	24 May	F	Dublin	England	3	Eire	1
	27 May	F	New York	England	10	USA	0
	30 May	T	Rio de Janeiro	England	1	Brazil	5
	4 June	T	Sao Paulo	England	1	Portugal	1
	6 June	T	Rio de Janeiro	England	0	Argentina	1
	3 October	HC	Belfast	England	4	N Ireland	3
	21 October	F	Wembley	England	2	Belgium	2
	18 November	HC	Wembley	England	2	Wales	1
	9 December	F	Amsterdam	England	1	Holland	1
1965	10 April	HC	Wembley	England	2	Scotland	2
	5 May	F	Wembley	England	1	Hungary	0
	9 May	F	Belgrade	England	1	Yugoslavia	1
	12 May	F	Nuremburg	England	1	W Germany	0
	16 May	F	Gothenburg	England	2	Sweden	1
	2 October	HC	Cardiff	England	0	Wales	0
	20 October	F	Wembley	England	2	Austria	3
	10 November	HC	Wembley	England	2	N Ireland	1
	8 December	F	Madrid	England	2	Spain	0
1966	5 January	F	Everton	England	1	Poland	1
	23 February	F	Wembley	England	1	W Germany	0
	2 April	HC	Glasgow	England	4	Scotland	3
	4 May	F	Wembley	England	2	Yugoslavia	0
	26 June	F	Helsinki	England	3	Finland	0
	29 June	F	Oslo	England	6	Norway	1
	3 July	F	Copenhagen	England	2	Denmark	0
	5 July	F	Chorzow	England	1	Poland	0
	11 July	WC	Wembley	England	0	Uruguay	0

YEAR	DATE	MATCH	VENUE	SCORE			
1966	16 July	WC	Wembley	England	2	Mexico	0
	20 July	WC	Wembley	England	2	France	0
	23 July	WC	Wembley	England	1	Argentina	0
	26 July	WC	Wembley	England	2	Portugal	1
	30 July	WC	Wembley	England	4	W Germany	2
	22 October	HC/ENC	Belfast	England	2	N Ireland	0
	2 November	F	Wembley	England	0	Czechoslovakia	0
	16 November	HC/ENC	Wembley	England	5	Wales	1
1967	15 April	HC/ENC	Wembley	England	2	Scotland	3
	24 May	F	Wembley	England	2	Spain	0
	27 May	F	Vienna	England	1	Austria	0
	21 October	HC/ENC	Cardiff	England	3	Wales	0
	22 November	HC/ENC	Wembley	England	2	N Ireland	0
1968	6 February	F	Wembley	England	2	USSR	2
	24 February	HC/ENC	Glasgow	England	1	Scotland	1
	3 April	ENC	Wembley	England	1	Spain	0
	8 May	ENC	Madrid	England	2	Spain	1
	22 May	F	Wembley	England	3	Sweden	1
	1 June	F	Hanover	England	0	W Germany	1
	5 June	ENC	Florence	England	0	Yugoslavia	1
	8 June	ENC	Rome	England	2	USSR	0
	6 November	F	Bucharest	England	0	Romania	0
	11 December	F	Wembley	England	1	Bulgaria	1
1969	15 January	F	Wembley	England	1	Romania	1
	12 March	F	Wembley	England	5	France	0
	3 May	HC	Belfast	England	3	N Ireland	1
	7 May	HC	Wembley	England	2	Wales	1
	10 May	HC	Wembley	England	4	Scotland	1
	1 June	F	Mexico City	England	0	Mexico	0
	8 June	F	Montevideo	England	2	Uruguay	1
	12 June	F	Rio de Janeiro	England	1	Brazil	2
	5 November	F	Amsterdam	England	1	Holland	0

Left: The programme for the England v Rest of the World meeting at Wembley in October 1963. The match, celebrating the centenary of the Football Association's foundation, ended in a 2-1 home victory.

10 JUNE 1984

England	2
Brazil	0
Venue: Rio de Janeiro	

England came to the home of Brazilian football, the famed Maracana Stadium in Rio, to teach the host nation a lesson in a friendly that would go down as one of England's all-time outstanding performances on foreign soil.

And the hero of the hour was Watford winger John Barnes, playing only his tenth international. He'd attacked the defence previously in the first half, but his solo run just before half-time was a mazy dribble that took him across field from his left-wing berth.

Beating defender after defender, he found himself one on one with keeper Costa and made no mistake with the scoring opportunity.

And Barnes it was in the second half who ensured England didn't let their advantage slip, centring after a Wilkins and Woodcock combination for centre-forward Mark Hateley to nod decisively home. Bobby Robson's decision to play two wingers, Mark Chamberlain of Stoke being the other, rather than pack the midfield had paid off handsomely.

If Barnes had taken a leaf out of Brazil's coaching manual for his first effort, this second and decisive strike was a typical English goal. Brazil were missing key players, but this detracted not one bit from a thrilling win.

England: Shilton, Duxbury, Sansom, Wilkins, Watson, Fenwick, Robson, Chamberlain, Hateley, Woodcock (Allen), Barnes.

Below: John Barnes, scorer of the spectacular goal in Rio that all England fans hark back to.

YEAR	DATE	MATCH	VENUE	SCORE			
1969	10 December	F	Wembley	England	1	Portugal	0
1970	14 January	F	Wembley	England	0	Holland	0
	25 February	F	Brussels	England	3	Belgium	1
	18 April	HC	Cardiff	England	1	Wales	1
	21 April	HC	Wembley	England	3	N Ireland	1
	25 April	HC	Glasgow	England	0	Scotland	0
	21 May	F	Bogotá	England	4	Colombia	0
	24 May	F	Quito	England	2	Ecuador	0
	2 June	WC	Guadalajara	England	1	Romania	0
	7 June	WC	Guadalajara	England	0	Brazil	1
	11 June	WC	Guadalajara	England	1	Czechoslovakia	0
	14 June	WC	León	England	2	W Germany	3
	25 November	F	Wembley	England	3	E Germany	1
1971	3 February	ECQ	Valletta	England	1	Malta	0
	21 April	ECQ	Wembley	England	3	Greece	0
	12 May	ECQ	Wembley	England	5	Malta	0
	15 May	HC	Belfast	England	1	N Ireland	0
	19 May	HC	Wembley	England	0	Wales	0
	22 May	HC	Wembley	England	3	Scotland	1
	13 October	ECQ	Basle	England	3	Switzerland	2
	10 November	ECQ	Wembley	England	1	Switzerland	1
	1 December	ECQ	Athens	England	2	Greece	0
1972	29 April	EC	Wembley	England	1	W Germany	3
	13 May	EC	Berlin	England	0	W Germany	0
	20 May	HC	Cardiff	England	3	Wales	0
	23 May	HC	Wembley	England	0	N Ireland	1
	27 May	HC	Glasgow	England	1	Scotland	0
	11 October	F	Wembley	England	1	Yugoslavia	1
	15 November	WCQ	Cardiff	England	1	Wales	0
1973	24 January	WCQ	Wembley	England	1	Wales	1
	14 February	F	Glasgow	England	5	Scotland	0
	12 May	HC	Everton	England	2	N Ireland	1
	15 May	HC	Wembley	England	3	Wales	0
	19 May	HC	Wembley	England	1	Scotland	0
	27 May	F	Prague	England	1	Czechoslovakia	1
	6 June	WCQ	Katowice	England	0	Poland	2
	10 June	F	Moscow	England	2	USSR	1
	14 June	F	Turin	England	0	Italy	2
	26 September	F	Wembley	England	7	Austria	0
	17 October	WCQ	Wembley	England	1	Poland	1
	14 November	F	Wembley	England	0	Italy	1
1974	3 April	F	Lisbon	England	0	Portugal	0
	11 May	HC	Cardiff	England	2	Wales	0
	15 May	HC	Wembley	England	1	N Ireland	0
	18 May	HC	Glasgow	England	0	Scotland	2
	22 May	F	Wembley	England	2	Argentina	2
	29 May	F	Leipzig	England	1	E Germany	1
	1 June	F	Sofia	England	1	Bulgaria	0
	5 June	F	Belgrade	England	2	Yugoslavia	2
	30 October	ECQ	Wembley	England	3	Czechoslovakia	0
	20 November	ECQ	Wembley	England	0	Portugal	0
1975	12 March	F	Wembley	England	2	W Germany	0
	16 April	ECQ	Wembley	England	5	Cyprus	0
	11 May	ECQ	Limassol	England	1	Cyprus	0
	17 May	HC	Belfast	England	0	N Ireland	0
	21 May	HC	Wembley	England	2	Wales	2

YEAR	DATE	MATCH	VENUE	SCORE			
1975	24 May	HC	Wembley	England	5	Scotland	1
	3 September	F	Basle	England	2	Switzerland	1
	30 October	ECQ	Bratislava	England	1	Czechoslovakia	2
	19 November	ECQ	Lisbon	England	1	Portugal	1
1976	24 March	F	Wrexham	England	2	Wales	1
	8 May	HC	Cardiff	England	1	Wales	0
	11 May	HC	Wembley	England	4	N Ireland	0
	14 May	HC	Glasgow	England	1	Scotland	2
	23 May	T	Los Angeles	England	0	Brazil	1
	28 May	T	New York	England	3	Italy	2
	13 June	WCQ	Helsinki	England	4	Finland	1
	8 September	F	Wembley	England	1	Eire	1
	13 October	WCQ	Wembley	England	2	Finland	1
	17 November	WCQ	Rome	England	0	Italy	2
1977	9 February	F	Wembley	England	0	Holland	2
	30 March	WCQ	Wembley	England	5	Luxembourg	0
	28 May	HC	Belfast	England	2	N Ireland	1
	31 May	HC	Wembley	England	0	Wales	1
	4 June	HC	Wembley	England	1	Scotland	2
	8 June	F	Rio de Janeiro	England	0	Brazil	0
	12 June	F	Buenos Aires	England	1	Argentina	1
	15 June	F	Montevideo	England	0	Uruguay	0
	7 September	F	Wembley	England	0	Switzerland	0
	12 October	WCQ	Luxembourg	England	2	Luxembourg	0
	16 November	WCQ	Wembley	England	2	Italy	0
1978	22 February	F	Munich	England	1	W Germany	2
	19 April	F	Wembley	England	1	Brazil	1
	13 May	HC	Cardiff	England	3	Wales	1
	16 May	HC	Wembley	England	1	N Ireland	0
	20 May	HC	Glasgow	England	1	Scotland	0
	24 May	F	Wembley	England	4	Hungary	1
	20 September	ECQ	Copenhagen	England	4	Denmark	3
	25 October	ECQ	Dublin	England	1	Eire	1
	29 November	F	Wembley	England	1	Czechoslovakia	0
1979	7 February	ECQ	Wembley	England	4	N Ireland	0
	19 May	HC	Belfast	England	2	N Ireland	0
	23 May	HC	Wembley	England	0	Wales	0
	26 May	HC	Wembley	England	3	Scotland	1
	6 June	ECQ	Sofia	England	3	Bulgaria	0
	10 June	F	Stockholm	England	0	Sweden	0
	13 June	F	Vienna	England	3	Austria	4
	9 September	ECQ	Wembley	England	1	Denmark	0
	17 October	ECQ	Belfast	England	5	N Ireland	1
	22 November	ECQ	Wembley	England	2	Bulgaria	0
1980	6 February	ECQ	Wembley	England	2	Eire	0
	26 March	F	Barcelona	England	2	Spain	0
	13 May	F	Wembley	England	3	Argentina	1
	17 May	HC	Wrexham	England	1	Wales	4
	20 May	HC	Wembley	England	1	N Ireland	1
	24 May	HC	Glasgow	England	2	Scotland	0
	31 May	F	Sydney	England	2	Australia	1
	12 June	EC	Turin	England	1	Belgium	1
	15 June	EC	Turin	England	0	Italy	1
	18 June	EC	Naples	England	2	Spain	1
	10 September	WCQ	Wembley	England	4	Norway	0
	15 October	WCQ	Bucharest	England	1	Romania	2

YEAR	DATE	MATCH	VENUE	SCORE			
1980	19 November	WCQ	Wembley	England	2	Switzerland	1
1981	25 March	F	Wembley	England	1	Spain	2
	29 April	WCQ	Wembley	England	0	Romania	0
	12 May	F	Wembley	England	0	Brazil	1
	20 May	HC	Wembley	England	0	Wales	0
	23 May	HC	Wembley	England	0	Scotland	1
	30 May	WCQ	Basle	England	1	Switzerland	2
	6 June	WCQ	Budapest	England	3	Hungary	1
	9 September	WCQ	Oslo	England	1	Norway	2
	18 November	WCQ	Wembley	England	1	Hungary	0
1982	23 February	HC	Wembley	England	4	N Ireland	0
	27 April	HC	Cardiff	England	1	Wales	0
	25 May	F	Wembley	England	2	Holland	0
	29 May	HC	Glasgow	England	1	Scotland	0
	2 June	F	Reykjavik	England	1	Iceland	1
	3 June	F	Helsinki	England	4	Finland	1
	16 June	WC	Bilbao	England	3	France	1
	20 June	WC	Bilbao	England	2	Czechoslovakia	0
	25 June	WC	Bilbao	England	1	Kuwait	0
	29 June	WC	Madrid	England	0	W Germany	0
	5 July	WC	Madrid	England	0	Spain	0
	22 September	ECQ	Copenhagen	England	2	Denmark	2
	13 October	F	Wembley	England	1	W Germany	2
	17 November	ECQ	Salonika	England	3	Greece	0
	15 December	ECQ	Wembley	England	9	Luxembourg	0
1983	23 February	HC	Wembley	England	2	Wales	1
	30 March	ECQ	Wembley	England	0	Greece	0
	27 April	ECQ	Wembley	England	2	Hungary	0
	28 May	HC	Belfast	England	0	N Ireland	0
	1 June	HC	Wembley	England	2	Scotland	0
	12 June	F	Sydney	England	0	Australia	0
	15 June	F	Brisbane	England	1	Australia	0
	19 June	F	Melbourne	England	1	Australia	1
	21 September	ECQ	Wembley	England	0	Denmark	1
	12 October	ECQ	Budapest	England	3	Hungary	0
	16 November	ECQ	Luxembourg	England	4	Luxembourg	0
1984	28 February	F	Paris	England	0	France	2
	4 April	HC	Wembley	England	1	N Ireland	0
	2 May	HC	Wrexham	England	0	Wales	1
	26 May	HC	Glasgow	England	1	Scotland	1
	2 June	F	Wembley	England	0	USSR	2
	10 June	F	Rio de Janeiro	England	2	Brazil	0
	13 June	F	Montevideo	England	0	Uruguay	2
	17 June	F	Santiago	England	0	Chile	0
	12 September	F	Wembley	England	1	E Germany	0
	17 October	WCQ	Wembley	England	5	Finland	0
	14 November	WCQ	Istanbul	England	8	Turkey	0
1985	26 February	WCQ	Belfast	England	1	N Ireland	0
	26 March	F	Wembley	England	2	Eire	1
	1 May	WCQ	Bucharest	England	0	Romania	0
	22 May	WCQ	Helsinki	England	1	Finland	1
	25 May	RC	Glasgow	England	0	Scotland	1
	6 June	T	Mexico City	England	1	Italy	2
	9 June	T	Mexico City	England	0	Mexico	1
	12 June	F	Mexico City	England	3	W Germany	0
	16 June	F	Los Angeles	England	5	USA	0

21 JUNE 1986

England	1
Argentina	2
Venue: Mexico City	

The Azteca Stadium in Mexico City, with over 100,000 fans inside, can justifiably be called one of world football's hotbeds. And with Argentina, Diego Maradona and all, this World Cup quarter-final was going to be the ultimate test of England's character. Bobby Robson's team selection showed caution, unlike the Brazil win two years previously, the aim obviously to stop the South Americans playing: Fenwick was soon in the book for a foul on Maradona.

It had little effect on the world's greatest player, however, as he proved five minutes after the restart. He played an inadvertent one-two off England's Steve Hodge, but Shilton looked favourite to punch clear as the ball ballooned up into the air. Yet it was the South American whose hand made contact, and the 'Hand of God' goal that resulted would go down in history.

England refused to let their heads drop, but another solo effort from Maradona, ironically rivalling John Barnes' 1984 wonder goal in brilliance, sealed the tie just four minutes later.

Gary Lineker's sixth goal of the competition with minutes left allowed England to leave the field with their heads held high, having completed a World Cup campaign by running the eventual World Champions as close as anyone. And besides, the score was really 1-1...

England: Shilton, Stevens, Sansom, Hoddle, Fenwick, Butcher, Hodge, Reid (Waddle), Beardsley, Lineker, Steven (Barnes).

YEAR	DATE	MATCH	VENUE	SCORE			
1985	11 September	WCQ	Wembley	England	1	Romania	1
	16 October	WCQ	Wembley	England	5	Turkey	0
	13 November	WCQ	Wembley	England	0	N Ireland	0
1986	29 January	F	Cairo	England	4	Egypt	0
	26 February	F	Tel Aviv	England	2	Israel	1
	26 March	F	Tbilisi	England	1	USSR	0
	23 April	RC	Wembley	England	2	Scotland	1
	17 May	F	Los Angeles	England	3	Mexico	0
	24 May	F	Vancouver	England	1	Canada	0
	3 June	WC	Monterrey	England	0	Portugal	1
	6 June	WC	Monterrey	England	0	Morocco	0
	11 June	WC	Monterrey	England	3	Poland	0
	18 June	WC	Mexico City	England	3	Paraguay	0
	21 June	WC	Mexico City	England	1	Argentina	2
	10 September	F	Stockholm	England	0	Sweden	1
	15 October	ECQ	Wembley	England	3	N Ireland	0
	12 November	ECQ	Wembley	England	2	Yugoslavia	0
1987	18 February	F	Madrid	England	4	Spain	2
	2 April	ECQ	Belfast	England	2	N Ireland	0
	29 April	ECQ	Izmir	England	0	Turkey	0
	19 May	RC	Wembley	England	1	Brazil	1
	23 May	RC	Glasgow	England	0	Scotland	0
	9 September	F	Düsseldorf	England	1	W Germany	3
	14 October	ECQ	Wembley	England	8	Turkey	0
	11 November	ECQ	Belgrade	England	4	Yugoslavia	1
1988	17 February	F	Tel Aviv	England	0	Israel	0
	23 March	F	Wembley	England	2	Holland	2
	27 April	F	Budapest	England	0	Hungary	0
	21 May	RC	Wembley	England	1	Scotland	0
	24 May	RC	Wembley	England	1	Colombia	1
	28 May	F	Lausanne	England	1	Switzerland	0
	12 June	EC	Stuttgart	England	0	Eire	1
	15 June	EC	Düsseldorf	England	1	Holland	3
	18 June	EC	Frankfurt	England	1	USSR	3
	14 September	F	Wembley	England	1	Denmark	0

YEAR	DATE	MATCH	VENUE	SCORE			
1988	19 October	WCQ	Wembley	England	0	Sweden	0
	16 November	F	Riyadh	England	1	Saudi Arabia	1
1989	8 February	F	Athens	England	2	Greece	1
	8 March	WCQ	Tirana	England	2	Albania	0
	26 April	WCQ	Wembley	England	5	Albania	0
	23 May	RC	Wembley	England	0	Chile	0
	27 May	RC	Glasgow	England	2	Scotland	0
	3 June	WCQ	Wembley	England	3	Poland	0
	7 June	F	Copenhagen	England	1	Denmark	1
	6 September	WCQ	Stockholm	England	0	Sweden	0
	11 October	WCQ	Katowice	England	0	Poland	0
	15 November	F	Wembley	England	0	Italy	0
	13 December	F	Wembley	England	2	Yugoslavia	1
1990	28 March	F	Wembley	England	1	Brazil	0
	25 April	F	Wembley	England	4	Czechoslovakia	2

Left: Trevor Steven, winner of 36 England caps, was replaced by John Barnes in the 1986 match against Argentina.

1 JULY 1990

England	3
Cameroon	2
Venue: Naples	

Anyone who ignores the emergence of the African nations as major forces in the football world does so at their peril. And though Cameroon had already shown their skills by reaching the World Cup quarter-final, they surprised England – and the world – by coming within an ace of a semi-final berth that will one day surely be theirs.

England, though, showed commendable team spirit in overcoming their green-shirted opponents, building on their last-gasp win against Belgium and refusing to let go. Yet all had looked plain sailing when Platt, the hero of the Belgium game, headed a Pearce cross past N'Kono.

Cameroon equalised ten minutes after the break from the penalty spot, Gascoigne having felled veteran folk-hero striker Roger Milla. Ekeke added a second and the traffic was all one way towards Shilton's net.

But the excitement was far from over, and another penalty decision, earned and converted by Lineker, pulled England back from the abyss with just eight minutes remaining.

Extra time saw the third penalty award of an absorbing game – and again Lineker was equal to the task, despite the pressure. He

hadn't had much practice, England having waited four years since their last spot-kick award, but his success set up a semi-final against old enemies West Germany.

Lineker again converted as the first man up in the penalty shoot-out, but Pearce and Waddle failed with their kicks, consigning Bobby Robson's men to the third-place play-off with host nation Italy.

England: Shilton, Parker, Pearce, Wright, Walker, Butcher (Steven), Platt, Waddle, Gascoigne, Lineker, Barnes (Beardsley).

Right: Cameroon's Omam Biyik hurdles England custodian Peter Shilton during the 1990 quarter-final.

YEAR	DATE	MATCH	VENUE	SCORE			
1990	15 May	F	Wembley	England	1	Denmark	0
	22 May	F	Wembley	England	1	Uruguay	2
	2 June	F	Tunis	England	1	Tunisia	1
	11 June	WC	Cagliari	England	1	Eire	1
	16 June	WC	Cagliari	England	0	Holland	0
	21 June	WC	Cagliari	England	1	Egypt	0
	26 June	WC	Bologna	England	1	Belgium	0
	1 July	WC	Naples	England	3	Cameroon	2
	4 July	WC	Turin	England	1	W Germany*	1
	7 July	WC	Bari	England	1	Italy	2
	12 September	F	Wembley	England	1	Hungary	0
	17 October	ECQ	Wembley	England	2	Poland	0
	14 November	ECQ	Dublin	England	1	Eire	1
1991	6 February	F	Wembley	England	2	Cameroon	0
	27 March	ECQ	Wembley	England	1	Eire	1
	1 May	ECQ	Izmir	England	1	Turkey	0
	21 May	ECC	Wembley	England	3	USSR	1
	25 May	ECC	Wembley	England	2	Argentina	2

YEAR	DATE	MATCH	VENUE	SCORE			
1991	1 June	F	Sydney	England	1	Australia	0
	3 June	F	Auckland	England	1	New Zealand	0
	8 June	F	Wellington	England	2	New Zealand	0
	12 June	F	Kuala Lumpur	England	4	Malaysia	2
	11 September	F	Wembley	England	0	Germany	1
	16 October	ECQ	Wembley	England	1	Turkey	0
	13 November	ECQ	Poznan	England	1	Poland	1
1992	19 February	F	Wembley	England	2	France	0
	25 March	F	Prague	England	2	Czechoslovakia	2
	29 April	F	Moscow	England	2	CIS	2
	12 May	F	Budapest	England	1	Hungary	0
	17 May	F	Wembley	England	1	Brazil	1
	3 June	F	Helsinki	England	2	Finland	1
	11 June	EC	Malmö	England	0	Denmark	0
	14 June	EC	Malmö	England	0	France	0
	17 June	EC	Stockholm	England	1	Sweden	2
	9 September	F	Santander	England	0	Spain	1
	14 October	WCQ	Wembley	England	1	Norway	1
	18 November	WCQ	Wembley	England	4	Turkey	0
1993	17 February	WCQ	Wembley	England	6	San Marino	0
	31 March	WCQ	Izmir	England	2	Turkey	0
	28 April	WCQ	Wembley	England	2	Holland	2
	29 May	WCQ	Katowice	England	1	Poland	1
	2 June	WCQ	Oslo	England	0	Norway	2
	9 June	USC	Boston	England	0	USA	2
	13 June	USC	Washington	England	1	Brazil	1
	19 June	USC	Detroit	England	1	Germany	2
	8 September	WCQ	Wembley	England	3	Poland	0
	13 October	WCQ	Rotterdam	England	0	Holland	2
	17 November	WCQ	Bologna	England	7	San Marino	1
1994	9 March	F	Wembley	England	1	Denmark	0
	17 May	F	Wembley	England	5	Greece	0
	22 May	F	Wembley	England	0	Norway	0
	7 September	F	Wembley	England	2	USA	0
	12 October	F	Wembley	England	1	Romania	1
	16 November	F	Wembley	England	1	Nigeria	0
1995	15 February	F	Dublin	England	0	Eire	1
	Abandoned after 27 minutes due to crowd trouble						
	29 March	F	Wembley	England	0	Uruguay	0
	3 June	UIT	Wembley	England	2	Japan	1
	8 June	UIT	Leeds	England	3	Sweden	3
	11 June	UIT	Wembley	England	1	Brazil	3
	6 September	F	Wembley	England	0	Colombia	0
	11 October	F	Oslo	England	0	Norway	0
	15 November	F	Wembley	England	3	Switzerland	1
	12 December	F	Wembley	England	1	Portugal	1

KEY:

WC	World Cup	UIT	Umbro International Trophy
WCQ	World Cup Qualifier	USC	US Cup
ENC	European Nations Cup	F	Friendly
EC	European Championship	•	England played two international
ECQ	EC Qualifier		matches on the same day, with the
HC	Home Championship		Corinthian Casuals asked to field
ECC	England Challenge Cup		teams to play Wales
RC	Rous Cup	*	Won the penalty shoot-out
T	Tournament		

ENGLAND'S RECORD SINCE THE 1966 WORLD CUP (CORRECT TO 31 DECEMBER 1995)

England v	P	W	D	L	F	A
Albania	2	2	—	—	7	—
Argentina	5	1	3	1	9	8
Australia	5	3	2	—	5	2
Austria	3	2	—	1	11	4
Belgium	3	2	1	—	5	2
Brazil	12	2	5	5	9	12
Bulgaria	4	3	1	—	7	1
Cameroon	2	2	—	—	5	2
Canada	1	1	—	—	1	—
Chile	2	—	2	—	—	—
CIS	1	—	1	—	2	2
Colombia	3	1	2	—	5	1
Cyprus	2	2	—	—	6	—
Czechoslovakia	9	5	3	1	15	7
Denmark	9	5	3	1	11	7
East Germany	3	2	1	—	5	2
Ecuador	1	1	—	—	2	—
Egypt	2	2	—	—	5	—
Eire	8	2	5	1	9	7
Finland	6	5	1	—	17	5
France	5	3	1	1	10	3
Germany	2	—	—	2	1	3
Greece	6	5	1	—	15	1
Holland	9	2	4	3	8	11
Hungary	8	7	1	—	15	2
Iceland	1	—	1	—	1	1
Israel	2	1	1	—	2	1
Italy	9	2	1	6	7	12
Japan	1	1	—	—	2	1
Kuwait	1	1	—	—	1	—
Luxembourg	4	4	—	—	20	—
Malaysia	1	1	—	—	4	2
Malta	2	2	—	—	6	—
Mexico	3	1	1	1	3	1
Morocco	1	—	1	—	—	—
New Zealand	2	2	—	—	3	—
Nigeria	1	1	—	—	1	—
Northern Ireland	23	18	4	1	44	7
Norway	6	1	3	2	6	5
Paraguay	1	1	—	—	3	—
Poland	9	4	4	1	14	5
Portugal	6	1	4	1	3	3
Romania	8	1	6	1	5	5
San Marino	2	2	—	—	13	1
Saudi Arabia	1	—	1	—	1	1
Scotland	24	14	4	6	39	18
Spain	9	6	1	2	14	7
Sweden	7	1	4	2	7	7
Switzerland	8	5	2	1	13	8
Tunisia	1	—	1	—	1	1
Turkey	8	7	1	—	29	—
Uruguay	5	1	2	2	3	5
USA	3	2	—	1	7	2
USSR	7	4	1	2	11	9
Wales	21	12	6	3	33	15
West Germany	11	2	3*	6	12	15
Yugoslavia	6	3	2	1	11	6

* Includes a 1-1 draw won on penalties by West Germany

Top: The programme for the Rous Cup clash with Brazil in 1987 which ended 1-1.

Above: Bryan Robson, England captain for the majority of the 1980s, in action.

3: MANAGERS

WALTER WINTERBOTTOM
1946-62

Though Walter Winterbottom technically presided over England's fortunes from the first postwar international onwards, he shouldn't be accorded all the blame – or praise! He started the 1946 season as Director of Coaching, only after that becoming national team manager too; but in the latter role he was merely part of a selection committee and could often be overruled by force of numbers.

Hailing from Oldham, he'd had a promising playing career with nearby Manchester United effectively ended by a combination of the war and chronic back problems. The impetus for his appointment, and the team manager's job, came from FA secretary Stanley Rous.

Winterbottom was, however, to preside over such humblings as the 1950 World Cup defeat at the hands of the United States and the Hungary reverses that underlined England's declining status in the world game. Even then, though, pundit-to-be Jimmy Hill realised the position was a thankless one. 'Walter is a talented and honourable man who deserves to succeed,' he said in 1961. 'Unfortunately he has chosen possibly the most difficult job in England.'

Winterbottom led England into four World Cups, but failed to do more than reach the quarter-finals in any. It's inconceivable that a manager these days would be given so many chances, but for the last two at least he had a three-man committee – himself and two FA members – to pick the team. Outside that, he had to do everything himself, down to organising the travel arrangements: today's well-oiled administrative machine simply did not exist.

The statistics suggest that Walter Winterbottom's England won the majority of the games they played, scoring nearly double the number of goals that they conceded. So far, so good – but no silverware, nor any likelihood of it. True, the European Championship – or European Nations Cup, as it was originally known – was not yet an issue (England's first match in it was 1962), and this narrowed down his chances.

When he was defeated in a vote for FA secretary to replace Stanley Rous who was moving to FIFA after 27 years, Winterbottom moved on, later becoming director of the Sports Council and receiving a knighthood. On paper, his record as the first England manager doesn't look outstanding, but successors Alf Ramsey and Ron Greenwood both believed him to be influential on the tactical structure of the game.

ENGLAND RECORD

P	W	D	L	F	A	Success Rate
138	78	31	29	383	197	68%

39

SIR ALF RAMSEY
1963-74

When it comes to selecting England's most successful manager ever, few would look further than one man – Alfred Ernest Ramsey. His motivation was undoubted, and stemmed from the shame of being on the Wembley pitch when Hungary had handed English football an object lesson back in 1953.

'I have had one great ambition hanging over me for years, to replace the image of that great Hungarian team by the image of an even greater England team.'

Born in Dagenham, Essex, in 1920, he'd made his England début as a player in 1948, the year before he left his first professional club Southampton for Spurs in a £21,000 deal. The London club bought seven years of sterling service, 250 League and Cup games which included 24 goals – mostly penalties.

Early days at Portman Road, Ipswich, in his first job in 1955 were uncomfortable, but he emerged from the shadow of predecessor Scott Duncan (who was still on the scene, having been appointed secretary) with the Third Division (South) title in 1957, followed by the Second and First in consecutive seasons 1960-62. He never paid more than £12,500 for a player, a fact that underlined his man-management skills. Outwardly calm and unassuming, a steely determination lay beneath the veneer.

Having taken Ipswich from Third Division strugglers to the League Championship in five years, Ramsey needed just three to crown his England tenure with the World title. As at Ipswich he demanded and was given full overall control of selection and preparation. His tactic of choosing players to fit a system meant that talented individuals sometimes missed out, but the results stifled criticism.

In the World Cup he left out master goalscorer Jimmy Greaves from the quarter-finals onwards – a tactic that, had his replacement Geoff Hurst not covered himself in glory, might have brought the wrath of the press down on him. But aside from an opening 0-0 draw against Uruguay England's games were all memorable, even the match against Argentina whom Ramsey uncharacteristically described as 'animals'.

He was fiercely loyal to his own players, and received the same dedication in return – a trait that served England well when picking themselves up from a last-gasp West German equaliser. 'You've beaten them once – now go out and beat them again,' said Ramsey to players who would have run through a brick wall for their boss. It was the kind of loyalty his successor Don Revie tried and failed to emulate.

Knighted the year after his triumph, he would take England into two more World Cup campaigns and two European Championships. The first of the latter brought third place in 1968, but a disastrous quarter-final loss to West Germany in Mexico '70 after being two goals up burst the bubble. Ramsey's double substitution preceding the slide may or may not have affected the course of the game, but it was certain that England no longer ruled the world.

The Germans made it the best of three when they eliminated England from the European Championship two years later. A 3-1 defeat at Wembley left them with all to do in Berlin, where the game ended goalless and Ramsey's tactical naïvety was called into question.

The 1970s would belong to 'total football' teams like Germany and Holland, not Ramsey's rigid formations, and when Poland blocked England's path to the West German World Cup in 1973 he was dismissed, albeit with a glowing testimony.

Having joined the board of Birmingham City, Ramsey returned briefly to management in 1977, but – in his late 50s – was afflicted with ill-health and gave up the position after just six months. He has since

returned to East Anglia, scene of his earlier club triumphs, to enjoy retirement.

Time, not to mention the lack of subsequent silverware brought home by his successors, has shown Alf Ramsey to be England's outstanding manager to date. His 4-4-2 formation, dubbed the 'wingless wonders' by the press, with hard-working midfielders preferred to out-and-out wide men, became the most common team line-up. And with only 17 out of 113 games lost, his statistics are impressive too.

Left: Alf Ramsey with his national squad during training in 1965, the year before his greatest triumph.

Above: Ramsey's credentials for the England job included three Divisional titles with Ipswich.

CLUB RECORD

CLUB	FROM	TO
Ipswich Town	August 1955	January 1963
Birmingham City	September 1977	March 1978
HONOURS		
Division One Champions:		1961-62
Division Two Champions:		1960-61
Division Three (South) Champions:		1956-57

ENGLAND RECORD

P	W	D	L	F	A	Success Rate
113	69	27	17	224	98	73%

JOE MERCER
1974

Legend has it that when Joe Mercer walked into the Football Association offices in 1974 to discuss his forthcoming tenure as caretaker manager, the receptionist asked if he had an appointment. 'Yes, love,' he smiled. 'For seven matches...'

Apocryphal or not, the exchange sums up both the nature of the man and his connection with the England manager's job. Because he knew he was only a stop-gap, there was no pressure involved: he would lead his country through the Home Internationals and the summer tour that followed, then give way to the FA's chosen appointee.

The results obtained suggest that a series of short-term managers could be the answer to England's problems: under Mercer's guidance, they won three, drew three and lost only one. Even better, from the FA's point of view, his popular appointment eased criticism of their sacking of Alf Ramsey which, had it been followed by the controversial appointment of Don Revie – already in the frame at this stage – would have been all the louder.

Born in 1914, Joe Mercer had enjoyed a long and distinguished playing career with Everton (1931-39) and Arsenal (1946-54), before entering club management with Sheffield United. His playing career had seen him win three League Championships and play in two FA Cup Finals, as well as five peacetime caps for England. Most of that success had come with Arsenal whom he joined in his 30s when many had written him off through age and a knee injury; this was clearly a man of some determination. He played on at the highest level until breaking a leg within sight of his 40th birthday.

His spell at debt-ridden Villa was unhappy: he suffered a stroke through overwork and the club barely waited for his recovery before sacking him. Not for the first time Mercer had the last laugh, winning the League, Cup, League Cup and Cup Winners' Cup at Maine Road where the younger Malcolm Allison was his 'legs'. A similar arrangement at Coventry from 1972-74 with Gordon Milne proved less successful.

Wales and Northern Ireland were beaten, but Scotland proved too strong at Hampden. A Wembley friendly against Argentina finished all-square, as did visits to East Germany and Yugoslavia; Bulgaria were beaten by a goal from Frank Worthington, one of the flair players who responded to Mercer's direction.

Joe Mercer left the England job to enjoy a well-earned retirement on his native Merseyside until his death in 1990.

CLUB RECORD

CLUB	FROM	TO
Sheffield Utd	August 1955	December 1958
Aston Villa	December 1958	July 1964
Manchester C	July 1965	October 1971

HONOURS	
Division One Champions:	1967-68
Division Two Champions:	1959-60, 1965-66
FA Cup Winners:	1969
League Cup Winners:	1961, 1970
League Cup Runners-up:	1963
European Cup Winners' Cup Winners:	1969-70

ENGLAND RECORD

P	W	D	L	F	A	Success Rate
7	3	3	1	9	7	64%

DON REVIE
1974-77

Writing in *FA News* just before the 1966 World Cup, Leeds manager Don Revie said: 'If England win, it would be the greatest thrill of this season for me – but sadly I cannot see them doing so.'

It was a rare miscalculation from a man who, at club level, created a team that were respected by some and feared by all for their uncompromising football. But Revie's next mistake was to take the national job in 1974, little realising that his intense style so successful with Leeds would not translate to players he met somewhat less regularly and whose devotion was to say the least variable.

As a player Revie had proved himself a master tactician, winning six full caps in a career that started with Leicester in 1944 but, after a spell with Hull City, bloomed in the 1950s at Maine Road, Manchester. His deeply-lying centre-forward role, Hungarian-style, bamboozled domestic defences and gave him 1955's Footballer of the Year crown. He reached Leeds via Sunderland in 1958, becoming player-manager three years later and hanging up his boots in 1963.

Two League crowns and one FA Cup win followed their 1964 promotion to the top flight, but five second places and three losing Finals show what might have been. They did well in Europe too, winning the Fairs (now UEFA) Cup in 1968 and 1971, reaching two more European Finals, before Revie took the England job.

Revie's safety-first style and habit of producing dossiers on the opposition, added to a new system of financial motivation for the players, backfired drastically. He rarely chose a settled side – two different games against Wales in 1976 saw 11 new caps – and even when he relied on the backbone of five players from Liverpool, the outstanding club of the era, couldn't seem to get it right.

The World Cup qualification battle had been all but lost when he quit, though Ron Greenwood put out a team that beat table-topping Italy – a victory in the third game of his trial period which gave him the job permanently. Don Revie never re-entered the English game as a club manager, though he successfully fought the FA ban that prohibited him from doing so after taking a coaching job with the United Arab Emirates.

He died in May 1989, after a long battle against motor neurone disease, asking that his ashes be strewn over the Elland Road pitch.

CLUB RECORD

CLUB	FROM	TO
Leeds United	March 1961	July 1974

HONOURS

Division One Champions:	1968-69, 1973-74
Division One Runners-up:	1964-65, 1965-66, 1969-70, 1970-71, 1971-72
Division Two Champions:	1963-64
FA Cup Winners:	1972
FA Cup Runners-up:	1965, 1970, 1973
League Cup Winners:	1968
European Cup Winners' Cup Runners-up:	1972-73
European Fairs (UEFA) Cup Winners:	1967-68, 1970-71
European Fairs (UEFA) Cup Runners-up:	1966-67

ENGLAND RECORD

P	W	D	L	F	A	Success Rate
29	14	8	7	49	25	62%

RON GREENWOOD
1977-82

Though he only acceded to the 'throne' in 1977, Ron Greenwood had already been informally approached when a successor to Walter Winterbottom was sought a decade and a half earlier. He later admitted the fact that this early approach came to nothing was 'a blessing in disguise', adding with typical frankness: 'I wasn't ready for it, while Alf Ramsey certainly was.'

The fact that the intervening years were spent at one club, West Ham, clearly weighed highly when the FA were looking for a man of integrity to replace the discredited Don Revie. Since 1974, he'd ceded control of the team to protégé John Lyall, and at 55 still had a few good years left in him. What was more, he'd already been involved in the England set-up when, in the late 1950s, he helped his friend Walter Winterbottom by running the national Youth and Under-23 sides for some two and a half years.

Though born in Burnley in 1921, Greenwood spent most of his playing and managerial career in the capital. Emerging at Chelsea during the war years, he moved to Bradford City seeking first-team football but enjoyed his best days with Brentford from 1949-52 where he gained B international recognition. Spells at Chelsea (again) and Fulham followed, before a managerial apprenticeship at Walthamstow, Eastbourne and Arsenal (as assistant to George Swindin) laid the foundations for things to come.

Becoming just the fourth manager in West Ham's history in 1961, he led them to FA Cup and Cup Winners' Cup success in 1964 and 1965, but his attacking football policies were not otherwise reflected in silverware. West Ham did, however, supply England's World Cup team with its backbone of Moore, Hurst and Peters, while Greenwood himself served as technical adviser to FIFA for this and the following Finals.

Greenwood's England record was relatively successful, winning 33 of the 55 games played under his command and taking the national team to the Final stages of both the European Championship and World Cup before stepping down voluntarily after the latter in 1982. In terms of games he ranks fourth behind Winterbottom, Ramsey and Robson.

Ron Greenwood became a director of Brighton and Hove Albion in 1983, maintaining some contact in retirement with the game he loved.

CLUB RECORD

CLUB	FROM	TO
West Ham Utd	April 1961	August 1974
HONOURS		

FA Cup Winners:		1964
League Cup Runners-up:		1966
European Cup Winners' Cup Winners:		1964-65

ENGLAND RECORD

P	W	D	L	F	A	Success Rate
55	33	12	10	93	40	71%

BOBBY ROBSON
1982-90

Bobby Robson won 20 England caps as a player before becoming manager of his country. And though he failed to bring back the silverware in that position, his success at club level both before and after his tenure, not to mention the quarter and semi-final showings in the two World Cups into which he led his team, suggest he was Alf Ramsey's most notable successor.

Born in County Durham in 1933, Robson played for Fulham from 1950 to 1967, save for a six-year spell with West Bromwich from 1956-62. At Craven Cottage, he benefited from playing alongside fellow internationals Johnny Haynes and Bedford Jezzard, and was clearly a thinker. Encouraged to take up coaching by national manager Walter Winterbottom, he became an FA staff coach, and coached the Oxford University team from 1965 to 1966.

He returned to Fulham, this time as manager, in 1968, having meanwhile worked with Vancouver Royals in Canada, but this third spell proved less than successful. He was sacked after only ten months; too many of his players were former team-mates, making his job that much more difficult, and he had been too late to avert relegation from the First Division.

Ipswich appointed him successor to Bill McGarry in 1969, and he enjoyed 13 successful years in Suffolk, his first task another attempt – this time successful – to keep the club in the top flight. Working with limited resources, he took his side to second place in consecutive seasons 1980-82, the top four five times and the FA Cup in 1978. Biggest triumph was the UEFA Cup in 1981 with a team that included England players like Mick Mills, Terry Butcher and Paul Mariner.

His eight years in charge of the national side followed half that time served as part-time England B boss, and he qualified for three out of the four competitions (two World Cups, two European Championships) the senior side contested. Argentine striker Maradona's illegal but unspotted 'hand of God' goal was enough to knock England out of the 1986 World Cup, but the manner of the win (and, to be honest, Argentina's clear superiority when not cheating, was exemplified by Maradona's other goal) made

their quarter-final exit easier to bear than Alf Ramsey's team at the same stage in the same location 16 years earlier.

The biggest disappointment by far of Robson's management was the 1988 European Championship Finals, with Jack Charlton's Eire – composed of supposedly inferior players from the Football League – one of three teams to send England home empty-handed. Yet their other two opponents would win through to contest the Final. And they hadn't done badly compared with four years previously, when a single-goal home defeat at Wembley by Denmark had scuppered their chances of reaching the Final stages at all. That result, while poorly received, was as nothing to the headlines to greet the team on their return this time.

Robson was the first England manager to undergo 'trial by tabloid', one of the newspapers even offering its readers 'Robson out' lapel badges. Though pursued by Barcelona, he refused to give in to certain loudly expressed sections of public opinion and persevered: the man he recommended in

Left: Bobby Robson, pictured during the 1990 World Cup in Italy where he led England to the semi-finals. It is the closest any manager has come to emulating Sir Alf Ramsey's 1966 success.

his stead was, incidentally, Terry Venables.

He had already decided to step down after the 1990 World Cup Finals, but bowed out on a high – the so near yet so far semi-final with West Germany, decided on penalties after a 1-1 extra-time scoreline. Robson's reign had seen such talents as Lineker and Gascoigne grace the international stage, and it was no surprise when he found further success at club level with PSV Eindhoven in Holland (where he won the domestic title in his first season) and Portugal's Porto, where he exacted revenge on previous charges Sporting Lisbon, emerging victorious from the 1993-94 Cup Final and seeing his side crowned League Champions the following season.

Robson's statistical record reflects a tight defence, marshalled by record-breaking goalkeeper Peter Shilton, with just 60 goals conceded in 95 games. But a record of just one and a half goals scored per game suggests that another proven goal-poacher alongside golden boy Gary Lineker could have made all the difference…especially in that fated semi-final!

CLUB RECORD

CLUB	FROM	TO
Vancouver Royals	May 1967	January 1968
Fulham	January 1968	November 1968
Ipswich Town	January 1969	July 1982
PSV Eindhoven	August 1990	May 1992
Sporting Lisbon	May 1992	December 1993
FC Porto	February 1994	
HONOURS		
Division One Runners-up:		1980-81, 1981-82
FA Cup Winners:		1978
UEFA Cup Winners:		1980-81

ENGLAND RECORD

P	W	D	L	F	A	Success Rate
95	47	30*	18	154	60	65%

* Includes a 1-1 draw which West Germany won on penalties

GRAHAM TAYLOR
1990-94

Graham Taylor was the first manager the FA had to pay a transfer fee for: he'd still a year of his Aston Villa contract to run when the England job offer was made, and £225,000 changed hands to secure his services. Lawrie McMenemy, the former Southampton manager, was installed as his number two, but even with such an experienced hand on board and a track record with the Youth, Under 21 and B teams, Taylor's tenure was to be a troubled one.

Ten years of professional football as a full-back at grass-roots level with Grimsby and Lincoln had groomed Taylor to take the helm at Sincil Bank in late 1972. Five years later, Watford came in for him and his decade at Vicarage Road was to boost his – and their – profile immeasurably. Within six years of his arrival, he'd taken them from the Fourth Division to runner's-up position in the top flight. Three good Cup runs culminated in a Final appearance against Everton in 1984.

Three years later he decided to accept the challenge of revitalising Aston Villa, European Cup winners earlier in the decade but then in the Second Division. He returned them to the top flight in his first season, and in 1990 they finished runners-up to Liverpool – perfect timing to put him in the frame for the national job.

Taylor's team remained undefeated until September 1991 – a record start for any England manager – but new caps like Geoff Thomas, Mark Walters, Andy Gray, Brian Deane and, initially at least, Dennis Wise, seemed unable to meet the standard required. The 1992 European Championship Finals were reached, thanks to a Lineker-inspired draw in Poland, but the team's performance there was unsatisfactory: two draws and a defeat.

The qualifying games for the 1994 World Cup proved too high a hurdle for Taylor's squad. Defeat against Norway in the Ullevaal Stadium left them chasing the pack, needing to win all three remaining games and hoping someone would slip up.

Even lowly San Marino managed to open the scoring against England after just nine seconds (the quickest goal ever in international football), underlining the feeling that Taylor's tactical chopping and changing had availed him little. He fell on his sword, and few mourned – though many regretted the tabloids' unjustifiable hate campaigns, one of the more bizarre of which involved turning him into a turnip.

Though Alf Ramsey would manage Birmingham City for a six-month period in the mid 1970s, Taylor was the only England manager to return in any permanent sense to the club scene from whence he'd came. And sadly his association with Wolves, which ended in December 1995, failed to last two years. In early 1996 he returned to Watford as general manager.

CLUB RECORD

CLUB	FROM	TO
Lincoln City	December 1972	June 1977
Watford	June 1977	July 1987
Aston Villa	July 1987	July 1990
Wolves	March 1994	December 1995

HONOURS	
Division One Runners-up:	1982-83, 1989-90
Division Two Runners-up:	1981-82, 1987-88
Division Three Runners-up:	1978-79
Division Four Champions:	1975-76, 1977-78
FA Cup Runners-up:	1984

ENGLAND RECORD

P	W	D	L	F	A	Success Rate
38	18	12	8	62	32	63%

TERRY VENABLES
1994-96

The England manager's job seemed tailor-made for Terry Venables – the only man to have represented England as a player at schoolboy, youth, amateur, Under 23 and full international level. Yet circumstances conspired to make his potentially the shortest permanent tenure on record. He announced in January 1996 that he would not be leading the national team beyond the European Championship due to legal complications and allegations about his business interests.

Venables, born in London in 1943, had been a popular choice to succeed Graham Taylor. His pedigree included a Spanish title with Barcelona in 1985 and a European Cup Final lost on penalties the following season, and his return to Britain to manage Tottenham Hotspur led to an FA Cup win in 1991. Two years later, however, he departed amid acrimonious exchanges with owner Alan Sugar, and the legal ramifications of this, plus libel suits against others who had pried into his business affairs, were among the reasons he gave for leaving the England job.

His playing career spanned four London clubs from 1958-76: Chelsea, Spurs, Queens Park Rangers and Crystal Palace. It was at the latter two, in reverse order, that he'd begun his stint in management. Two promotions with Palace led to his 'Team of the Eighties', but they flattered to deceive and Venables moved to complete a personal promotion hat-trick with QPR. They also reached the 1982 FA Cup Final while still in the Second Division.

Venables' first dozen matches with the England team from his 1994 appointment brought only one defeat, against Brazil in the Umbro International Trophy, but saw seven matches drawn. With qualification for Euro '96 assured as hosts, he evolved a 'Christmas tree' formation with Alan Shearer the sole striker – even though this courted the wrath of critics pushing the claims of rival spearheads like Les Ferdinand and Andy Cole. Teddy Sheringham, a Spurs player under Venables, and Peter Beardsley fed off Shearer, but the Blackburn man's inability to reproduce his deadly club form in a white shirt may have caused the preponderance of draws.

CLUB RECORD

CLUB	FROM	TO
Crystal Palace	June 1976	October 1980
QPR	October 1980	May 1984
Barcelona	May 1984	September 1987
Spurs	November 1987	July 1991
HONOURS		
Division Two Champions:		1978-79, 1982-83
Division Three Promotion:		1976-77
FA Cup Winners:		1991
FA Cup Runners-up:		1982

ENGLAND RECORD (TO END 1995)

P	W	D	L	F	A	Success Rate
14	6	7	1	19	10	68%

England will be playing at Wembley – but seven other grounds will host Euro '96

Wembley Stadium is the England national team's traditional home – a link both strengthened and confirmed by the 1966 World Cup win. A plaque commemorates that event. But when the stadium first opened for the 1923 FA Cup Final prior to the following year's Empire Exhibition, it was not the intention that it should be the England team's base. Until 1951, Wembley staged just one or two major football matches each season — the FA Cup Final, as it had since 1923, and the England-Scotland fixture in alternate years.

England's first internationals were played south of the river at a venue now known exclusively for its cricket connections – the Kennington Oval. The first out-of-capital game was staged in Blackburn in 1881, Liverpool and Sheffield following two years later.

Wembley's first taste of international action came with the visit of Scotland in April 1924, one year after its opening. Honours were even on that occasion, but the same fixture four years later – Wembley's second international – resulted in a crushing 1-5 home defeat and the birth of the 'Wembley Wizards' legend.

Wembley continued to be used for that annual fixture, alternating with Hampden Park every second year, until the war. Wartime internationals at the stadium included visits from Wales and, in 1945, the newly liberated France. Belgium came in a 1946 Victory International and then it was back to alternate years until 1951.

The stadium acquired a roof in 1963 at a cost of £500,000, using translucent fibreglass panels on the inner 36 feet of roofing to help cover all 100,000 patrons, 56,000 of whom stood.

These days, the stadium is wholly seated and, though its capacity was inevitably reduced as a consequence, every available space has been utilised. The Olympic Gallery runs around the entire stadium, broken only by a row of executive boxes on the Royal Box side and the television gantry and studio on the other.

Elsewhere, Wembley, which is on a site that now includes the Arena, Conference Centre and an hotel, has undergone a facelift that has brought it into the 1990s. Toilets and food outlets have been improved and refurbished, the owners having spent considerable sums bringing these amenities up to date. Road access, however, remains a problem.

A new national stadium may one day be built, Manchester or Birmingham being the

Below: Wembley, formerly known as the Empire Stadium, scene of England's World Cup triumph in 1966.

EURO '96 MATCHES AT WEMBLEY, LONDON

8 June	Group A	England	v	Switzerland
15 June	Group A	Scotland	v	England
18 June	Group A	Holland	v	England
22 June	Quarter-Final	Winner Group A	v	Runners-up Group B
26 June	Semi-Final	Winner (Wembley)	v	Winner (Old Trafford)
30 June	Final			

EURO '96 MATCHES AT ELLAND ROAD, LEEDS

9 June	Group B	Spain	v	Bulgaria
15 June	Group B	France	v	Spain
18 June	Group B	Romania	v	Spain
26 June	Semi-Final	Winner (Anfield)	v	Winner (Villa Park)

possible sites, but regardless of lottery funds it will take time for these plans to get off the drawing board – if indeed they ever do – and it will be difficult to replicate the tradition and romance of Wembley itself.

Regardless of Wembley's future, the stadium was to play host to England's Euro '96 campaign, not to mention the Final. Whether another plaque will be added to the one inspired by events 30 years earlier remains to be seen.

Villa Park, Birmingham, has been the home of Aston Villa since 1897, when a stadium was built on the site of the old Aston Lower Grounds amusement park. Its biggest changes were seen in 1966 with the staging of World Cup games when the Witton Lane Stand went all-seater, the pitch was extended

by three yards and 6,250 temporary seats appeared on the uncovered Witton End banking (in the late 1970s, this end was replaced by a new North Stand).

The 1922-vintage Trinity Road Stand was designed by celebrated football ground architect Archibald Leitch, while the Holte End banking, finished in late 1939, was belatedly covered in 1962. At the end of the 1993-94 season the Holte End — frequented by Villa's most vocal terrace fans — gave way to a two-tier stand. This, along with the New Witton Lane Stand, rebuilt on two levels at a cost of £5 million and named after

Below: The East Stand at Elland Road was opened two years after Leeds United returned to the top flight in 1990.

chairman Doug Ellis, made Villa Park an all-seater stadium with a capacity of 40,000.

In just over a decade, Leeds United's Elland Road ground has staged a Rugby League Test match, played host to Bradford City after the fire at Valley Parade and hosted the FA Vase Final replay; selection for the European Championship in 1996 is the crowning achievement.

When the club reached the First Division in 1924, Elland Road had a Main Stand on the west side, a covered terrace at the Elland Road End, a long stand on the Lowfields Road side and open terracing at the North (Kop) End. A new 4,000-seat West Stand was opened in August 1957 to replace its fire-gutted predecessor.

The success of Don Revie's Leeds teams from 1964 was to transform the ground. In 1968 the open Kop was replaced by a covered terraced stand, the pitch being shifted 30 feet so that one goal stood where the base of the old terracing had lain. The pitch was again moved northwards in 1974 when the 7,500-capacity South Stand was built.

In the 1989-90 season a 2,800-capacity family stand and boxes were built at a cost of £500,000; the south-east corner gained 1,300 seats in the summer of 1991, while the Lowfields Road Stand was replaced the following year by a 17,000 all-seater two-tiered East Stand boasting the largest cantilever roof span of any ground in Europe. The North Stand (Kop) was seated in 1994 at a cost of £1.1 million, adding a further

6,800 seats and completing an impressive venue of international standard.

While Goodison Park was the host when Merseyside staged World Cup games in 1966, the three intervening decades saw Anfield designated as the city's Euro '96 venue. The ground had been the venue in December 1995 for a play-off between Eire and Holland, emphasising its pre-eminent position.

Above right: Villa Park in August 1994 with the Holte End under reconstruction.

Right: Anfield, home of Liverpool FC.

EURO '96 MATCHES AT VILLA PARK, BIRMINGHAM

10 June	Group A	Holland	v	Scotland
13 June	Group A	Switzerland	v	Holland
18 June	Group A	Scotland	v	Switzerland
23 June	Quarter-Final	Winner Group D	v	Runners-up Group C

EURO '96 MATCHES AT ANFIELD, LIVERPOOL

11 June	Group C	Italy	v	Russia
14 June	Group C	Czech Republic	v	Italy
19 June	Group C	Russia	v	Czech Republic
22 June	Quarter-Final	Winner Group B	v	Runners-up Group A

EURO '96 MATCHES AT OLD TRAFFORD, MANCHESTER

9 June	Group C	Germany	v	Czech Republic
16 June	Group C	Russia	v	Germany
19 June	Group C	Italy	v	Germany
23 June	Quarter-Final	Winner Group C	v	Runners-up Group D

EURO '96 MATCHES AT ST JAMES' PARK, NEWCASTLE

10 June	Group B	Romania	v	France
13 June	Group B	Bulgaria	v	Romania
18 June	Group B	France	v	Bulgaria

The conversion of the Kop in the summer of 1994 into a 12,400 all-seater stand signalled the end of an era. The famous banking (named after the Spion Kop in South Africa, where many Merseyside soldiers perished in the Boer War) first emerged in 1906, and in 1928 was covered and extended to hold just under 30,000.

The arrival of legendary manager Bill Shankly in 1959 signalled big changes at Anfield. In 1963, a year after the club gained promotion to the top flight, the Kemlyn Road Stand was replaced by a 7,000 all-seater construction. Ten years later a new Main Stand was officially opened and new floodlighting installed.

A new entrance and ticket office, which projected from the Main Stand on to the car park, was opened in August 1979. During the next close season an underpitch heating system was laid and the paddock terrace in the Main Stand seated. In May 1982 work began on adding 4,000 seats to the terraced

Below: Old Trafford, three decades on from the 1966 World Cup tournament.

Anfield Road End, which gave the ground a capacity of 45,000 (21,850 seats).

In 1992, the club's 100th year, the Kemlyn Road Stand was renamed the Centenary Stand and given a second tier. A car park replaced the row of houses which had to be demolished to make way for the development.

Anfield's international history started as far back as 1883 when Everton were still tenants, England beating Ireland 7-0. More recently, the ground saw the crucial Wales v Scotland World Cup qualifier in 1977. Despite the Kop's redevelopment and Liverpool's inconsistent fortunes in the 1990s, there were clearly more great spectacles ahead.

Old Trafford, the home of Manchester United, has seen seen much action on the field in the half-century between wartime bombing and its development as an all-seater stadium. And though the ground's capacity decreased by around one third over the period, it remained a must for European Championship inclusion.

The ground's first development was

Right: Hillsborough has now taken all of the recommendations of the Taylor Report on board.

Below right: Newcastle's St James' Park.

funded in 1909 by a local brewer, Archibald Leitch supervising the construction of a multi-span roofed stand which was opened in February 1910. The late 1920s saw the extension of the multi-span roof and the United Road side standing area covered.

German bombers dropped two bombs on Old Trafford, damaging the Main Stand and the United Road terracing which forced United to take up temporary residence at Maine Road. A 120,000-capacity stadium was the dream, but it was the 1966 World Cup that brought greatest change. The United Road cover gave way to an impressive cantilever construction which allowed for expansion at both ends and catered for both seated and standing spectators, as well as including the first executive boxes at a British football ground.

Work converting every roof to cantilever construction started in 1978 with the Main Stand, continuing until 75 per cent of the ground was covered in this way in 1985. The following year also saw the replacement of pylons with roof-mounted floodlights.

The redevelopment of standing areas was undertaken over four years in the early 1990s, the jewel in the crown being the new totally seated Stretford End, unveiled at the beginning of the 1993-94 season. The visitors' end was finally seated in 1994 and the 'bowl' roof was continued to form a perfect ellipse. Finally, after the modernisation of dressing-room facilities led to the resiting of the players' tunnel between the Main Stand and the Stretford End, 1995-96 saw attendances

limited due to construction work as a third tier was added to the United Road Stand increasing overall capacity to 55,000.

St James' Park's selection as a venue for the 1996 European Championship makes belated amends for missing out on the World Cup 30 years earlier. Newcastle's ground had initially been named as a 1966 venue, but wrangling with the city planners over a lease left them out in the cold for the big event. The situation was not resolved until 1971, when new plans for the ground were approved by the council.

In 1987 the West Stand, built just after the turn of the century, was demolished. In its place rose the new £5 million Milburn Stand (named after the club's famous centre-forward). In 1993, as the club moved towards

EURO '96 MATCHES AT THE CITY GROUND, NOTTINGHAM

11 June	Group D	Turkey	v	Croatia
14 June	Group D	Portugal	v	Turkey
19 June	Group D	Croatia	v	Portugal

EURO '96 MATCHES AT HILLSBOROUGH, SHEFFIELD

9 June	Group D	Denmark	v	Portugal
16 June	Group D	Croatia	v	Denmark
19 June	Group D	Turkey	v	Denmark

meeting Taylor's all-seater requirements, the Leazes Terrace was demolished and replaced by the Sir John Hall Stand (11,100 seats). The following year, the Gallowgate Terrace was pulled down to make way for a new 11,000-seater Gallowgate Stand.

Though England will be playing exclusively at Wembley, St James' Park has seen the national team in action on no fewer than seven occasions, the first (England 6 Wales 0) in 1901. For Newcastle supporters still smarting at rivals Sunderland's Roker Park seeing World Cup action in 1966, the return of international football will be good news indeed.

The inclusion of the City Ground as a venue for the 1996 European Championship is reward for an ambitious £15 million all-seater redevelopment programme by Nottingham Forest.

The building of two new stands at the Trent and Bridgford Ends in 1994-95 completed the stadium alongside the Main (west) Stand and Executive (east) Stand on the sides of the City Ground.

A new East Stand had been built in 1958 and four years later improvements and re-roofing were carried out on the Main Stand. At this time there were only 6,500 seats in a capacity of 48,000, a further indication of the transformation the ground has undergone. On 24 August 1968, however, this stand was gutted by fire during a League match, all spectators happily escaping serious injury.

The new Executive Stand – a two-tiered structure with a row of executive boxes – replaced the old East Stand in 1980, funded by domestic and European success under Brian Clough. The ground's current capacity is 30,569 and this, together with the equally impressive Meadow Lane across the Trent, makes Nottingham one of England's best-equipped footballing cities.

Although Hillsborough has become synonymous with the tragedy which cost 96 Liverpool supporters their lives on 17 April 1989, Sheffield Wednesday's home remains one of our most imposing sporting venues. The Taylor Report that followed changed the face of football grounds countrywide – and nowhere was this more true than at Hillsborough, which had to become a model for the new safety standards.

Capacity shrunk as Wednesday strove to meet the Report's requirements. In 1991, 2,610 seats were put into the lower section of the West Stand at the Leppings Lane End and a new roof added. Over £1.5 million was spent giving the ageing South Stand a new roof and seating in 1992 (2,733 seats in the lower section and 4,638 seats in the upper section).

Seating for over 11,211 was installed in the Spion Kop in the summer of 1993, seven years after it had acquired a £1 million roof. The changes gave a capacity of 36,020 (in 1971, Hillsborough had been able to accommodate 60,000).

The unveiling of the large and impressive new North Stand in August 1961 by Sir Stanley Rous paved the way for Hillsborough as a 1966 World Cup venue. That decision inevitably led to more changes as the ground was updated for the event. A new West Stand was completed a year before the Finals, seating capacity was increased in the South Stand and a centre for the world's media was installed at the north end of the ground.

Whether or not the home favourites emerge victorious, it's certain that the summer of 1996 will serve up a football feast for the British public to enjoy – and the facilities at these eight grounds will help them do just that.

Left: The new Trent End at Nottingham Forest's City Ground.

TONY ADAMS

AGE:	29
BIRTHDATE:	10 OCTOBER 1966
BIRTHPLACE:	LONDON
HEIGHT:	6' 3"
WEIGHT:	13st 11lb

An imposing central defender and inspirational leader, Adams was an integral part of the Arsenal team that enjoyed nearly a decade of success under George Graham. His commanding defensive presence has made him a fixture both with Arsenal (from November 1983, the month after he turned 17) and England.

National manager Bobby Robson, who first selected Adams in 1987, marvelled that he had 'such great stature for someone so young' and nominated him as an England captain of the future. He went on to play a part in the European Championship, scoring against Yugoslavia in the qualifiers and against the USSR in the ill-fated Finals.

Adams survived unsavoury publicity in 1990-91 after a double blow of a three-match ban for a professional foul and a short spell behind bars for a drink-driving offence. Arsenal regarded the slate as wiped clean, but he was not requested to wear an England shirt the following season. Graham Taylor forgave and forgot, recalling him to play in all the 1992-93 World Cup qualifiers, and he's remained in favour with Terry Venables, who even re-created the Highbury pairing with Steve Bould for 1994 games against Greece and Norway – the latter in front of David Seaman.

Whatever his off-field problems, Adams has always, in his own words, 'tried to do a professional job, whatever the opposition and the circumstances.' Should David Platt's injuries rule him out of Euro '96, Adams will also provide the inspirational leadership on the pitch which he does with or without the armband.

CLUB LEAGUE RECORD
(to start of 1995-96 season)

SEASON	CLUB	APPS	GOALS
1983-84	Arsenal	3	—
1984-85	Arsenal	16	—
1985-86	Arsenal	10	—
1986-87	Arsenal	42	6
1987-88	Arsenal	39	2
1988-89	Arsenal	36	4
1989-90	Arsenal	38	5
1990-91	Arsenal	30	1
1991-92	Arsenal	35	2
1992-93	Arsenal	35	—
1993-94	Arsenal	35	—
1994-95	Arsenal	27	3
Total		**346**	**23**

ENGLAND RECORD
(to 31 December 1995)

SEASON	APPS	GOALS
1986-87	3	—
1987-88	11	3
1988-89	3	1
1989-90	—	—
1990-91	2	—
1991-92	—	—
1992-93	7	—
1993-94	5	—
1994-95	4	—
1995-96	4	—
Total	**39**	**4**

NICK BARMBY

AGE:	22
BIRTHDATE:	11 FEBRUARY 1974
BIRTHPLACE:	HULL
HEIGHT:	5' 7"
WEIGHT:	11st 4lb

Critics were quick to link the remarkable international advancement of Nicholas Jonathan Barmby to his previous acquaintance with national manager Terry Venables at Tottenham. To the player's credit, he blew such criticism out of the water with some spirited performances, and amazed the doubters by preferring Bryan Robson's just-promoted Middlesbrough to staying at White Hart Lane.

'I like to play through the middle in an orthodox striker's role, dropping off or spinning,' says the player who explains that's how Terry Venables played him when he was at Spurs. It also suited Venables as England manager to try the same system against Colombia and Norway – and though no goals resulted in either case it seemed inconceivable that Barmby would be out of the reckoning. And indeed, against Portugal, he played orthodox midfield behind the front two of Shearer and Ferdinand.

At club level, the £5 million move soon bore fruit with Middlesbrough, one of the

ENGLAND RECORD
(to 31 December 1995)

SEASON	APPS	GOALS
1994-95	2	—
1995-96	3	—
Total	**5**	**—**

CLUB LEAGUE RECORD
(to start of 1995-96 season)

SEASON	CLUB	APPS	GOALS
1991-92	Tottenham H	—	—
1992-93	Tottenham H	22	6
1993-94	Tottenham H	27	5
1994-95	Tottenham H	38	9
Total		**87**	**20**

surprises of the 1995-96 season, and the teaming of Barmby and Brazilian wonderkid Juninho drew full houses to the new Riverside Stadium. Bryan Robson isn't the only person to have noticed the similarity between Barmby and Peter Beardsley – 'Nick has the potential to be better' – so when the Newcastle player finally bows to Father Time, Barmby will have the time and space to make himself an England fixture in the same way. At just 22, Euro '96 was clearly just the beginning...

PETER BEARDSLEY

AGE:	35
BIRTHDATE:	18 JANUARY 1961
BIRTHPLACE:	NEWCASTLE
HEIGHT:	5' 8"
WEIGHT:	11st 7lb

The Newcastle-born striker is surely international football's answer to Cliff Richard – apparently ageless, appealing to new generations (of England managers) and a hit with whichever partner he performs.

Kevin Keegan brought him back to the north-east in 1993 claiming his 49-cap England career was far from over; few believed him. Yet as the player says, 'When I left Liverpool everybody thought I was finished. But then I had two good years at Everton and then, luckily, I've had two good years so far at Newcastle.'

Injuries to both cheekbones have eaten into his two most recent seasons, yet the player has never let such matters affect his confidence. His international career has been an on-off affair, beginning in Egypt with a January 1986 substitute appearance, just three months before the World Cup Finals, and he'd played just three full games before

being brought in to partner Gary Lineker (who rates Peter his perfect partner).

He remained a regular until 1991, when Graham Taylor discarded him after four games. Yet after a spell with Everton he regained his best form and his international place, the latter in March 1994. His goals-to-games ratio is poor for a striker, but he remains a fixture in the squad.

A folk-hero on Tyneside, his club future is assured. 'As long as Peter Beardsley wants to play for this club,' says Kevin Keegan, 'there will always be a place for him.'

ENGLAND RECORD
(to 31 December 1995)

SEASON	APPS	GOALS
1985-86	9	2
1986-87	6	—
1987-88	11	3
1988-89	8	2
1989-90	11	—
1990-91	4	1
1991-92	—	—
1992-93	—	—
1993-94	3	1
1994-95	5	—
1995-96	1	—
Total	**58**	**9**

CLUB LEAGUE RECORD
(to start of 1995-96 season)

SEASON	CLUB	APPS	GOALS
1979-80	Carlisle Utd	37	8
1980-81	Carlisle Utd	43	10
1981-82	Carlisle Utd	22	4
From Vancouver Whitecaps			
1982-83	Manchester Utd	—	—
From Vancouver Whitecaps			
1983-84	Newcastle Utd	35	20
1984-85	Newcastle Utd	38	17
1985-86	Newcastle Utd	42	19
1986-87	Newcastle Utd	32	5
1987-88	Liverpool	38	15
1988-89	Liverpool	37	10
1989-90	Liverpool	29	10
1990-91	Liverpool	27	11
1991-92	Everton	42	15
1992-93	Everton	39	10
1993-94	Newcastle Utd	35	21
1994-95	Newcastle Utd	34	12
Total		**530**	**187**

LES FERDINAND

AGE:	29
BIRTHDATE:	18 DECEMBER 1966
BIRTHPLACE:	LONDON
HEIGHT:	5' 11"
WEIGHT:	13st 5lb

In old-fashioned days before Christmas-tree formations were invented a centre-forward led the line, was dominant in the air and instilled fear and trepidation in those deputed to mark him. Newcastle was the natural home of such a player, and when Les Ferdinand moved to St James' Park in the summer of 1995 he found his natural environment.

Only Duncan Ferguson can approach Ferdinand in his fulfilment of the traditional centre-forward's role. Ferdinand came relatively late into professional football, signing from non-league Hayes in 1987, and went on to establish himself as Queens Park Rangers' first-choice striker – though not before they loaned him to Turkish club Besiktas to broaden his experience.

He'd topped Rangers' scoring charts for the last three seasons prior to his departure, so it was no surprise that Kevin Keegan paid £6 million to secure his services. With a multinational forward line completed by wingers Gillespie and Ginola, Keegan knew Ferdinand would have the ammunition to score even more goals and hopefully add an honour to a Turkish Cup-winners' medal he'd earned at Besiktas – his only silverware to date.

His England career began under Graham Taylor, his most successful spell seeing two goals in as many games during 1993-94. Yet subsequent chances were to prove limited due to Terry Venables' tactic of playing a lone striker up front with no wide men – a role tailored to Alan Shearer and one to which Ferdinand was unaccustomed. Playing the Newcastle man therefore meant reverting to a conventional front two, and this was tried unsuccessfully against Portugal. The people's choice had his chance, it was implied, and the pairing had been found incompatible.

Ferdinand's international prospects, then, would seem to be limited in the short term. Venables' successor may look more kindly upon a man many judges in the game believe is the most complete centre-forward England has produced in a long while.

ENGLAND RECORD
(to 31 December 1995)

SEASON	APPS	GOALS
1992-93	4	1
1993-94	2	2
1994-95	1	—
1995-96	1	—
Total	**8**	**3**

CLUB LEAGUE RECORD
(to start of 1995-96 season)

SEASON	CLUB	APPS	GOALS
1986-87	QPR	2	—
1987-88	QPR	1	—
1987-88	Brentford (loan)	3	—
1988-89	QPR	—	—
1988-89	Besiktas (loan)	n/k	n/k
1989-90	QPR	9	2
1990-91	QPR	18	8
1991-92	QPR	23	10
1992-93	QPR	37	20
1993-94	QPR	36	16
1994-95	QPR	37	24
Total		**166**	**80**

TIM FLOWERS

AGE:	29
BIRTHDATE:	3 FEBRUARY 1967
BIRTHPLACE:	KENILWORTH
HEIGHT:	6' 2"
WEIGHT:	14st 4lb

Blackburn's decision to up the record fee for a goalkeeper in November 1993 to £2.4 million raised many an eyebrow – but it's turned out to be one of Jack Walker's best pieces of business. Tim Flowers is as impressive between the posts as Alan Shearer, the man he followed from Southampton to Ewood Park, is in beating his opposite number.

A Midlander by birth, he was transferred from his first club Wolves in 1986 for just £70,000 and spent a season understudying the great Peter Shilton. Displacing Shilton's successor at the Dell, John Burridge, initially proved a problem, but Flowers has been a top-flight regular since 1989.

He made his international début in the US Cup game against Brazil in Washington in June 1993, and conceded just a single goal due to poor marking. Indeed, it took one of Flowers' specialities, a brilliant reflex save, in the final minutes to ensured England didn't come away empty-handed.

After just one cap the following season, a shut-out against Greece, he staked his claim through the excellence of his club form. The majority of his England caps to date were won during Blackburn's Championship season. Sixteen clean sheets in the League campaign provided a solid foundation for success, and though keeping concentration was his biggest problem in some games, he was rarely found wanting.

Flowers is unfortunate to have David Seaman barring his way, and Ian Walker snapping at his heels. Less unflappable than the man in possession, he would nonetheless walk into most other international teams, and his time may come.

CLUB LEAGUE RECORD
(to start of 1995-96 season)

SEASON	CLUB	APPS	GOALS
1984-85	Wolves	38	—
1985-86	Wolves	25	—
1985-86	Southampton (loan)	—	—
1986-87	Southampton	9	—
1986-87	Swindon T (loan)	2	—
1987-88	Southampton	9	—
1987-88	Swindon T (loan)	5	—
1988-89	Southampton	7	—
1989-90	Southampton	35	—
1990-91	Southampton	37	—
1991-92	Southampton	41	—
1992-93	Southampton	42	—
1993-94	Southampton	12	—
1993-94	Blackburn R	29	—
1994-95	Blackburn R	39	—
Total		**330**	**—**

ENGLAND RECORD
(to 31 December 1995)

SEASON	APPS	GOALS
1992-93	1	—
1993-94	1	—
1994-95	5	—
1995-96	—	—
Total	**7**	**—**

PAUL GASCOIGNE

AGE:	29
BIRTHDATE:	27 MAY 1967
BIRTHPLACE:	GATESHEAD
HEIGHT:	5' 10"
WEIGHT:	11st 7lb

CLUB LEAGUE RECORD
(to start of 1995-96 season)

SEASON	CLUB	APPS	GOALS
1984-85	Newcastle Utd	2	—
1985-86	Newcastle Utd	31	9
1986-87	Newcastle Utd	24	5
1987-88	Newcastle Utd	35	7
1988-89	Tottenham H	32	6
1989-90	Tottenham H	34	6
1990-91	Tottenham H	26	7
1991-92	Tottenham H	—	—
1992-93	Lazio	22	4
1993-94	Lazio	17	2
1994-95	Lazio	2	—
Total		**225**	**46**

Gazza – five innocent letters that represent an enigma. Beloved of the national team's supporters ever since he wept in the 1990 World Cup semi-final, he's since caused tears of frustration and/or laughter to millions more.

Only one season, the World Cup year of 1989-90, has seen Gascoigne make more than a handful of appearances, yet that was originally Bobby Robson's plan. He rationed the player's appearances to avoid over-exposure, believing rightly that publicity might not be in the player's best interests. The build-up worked perfectly...yet the 1990 World Cup Finals remain Gascoigne's peak.

A blank year for club and country in 1991-92 followed a rash Cup Final challenge that ruptured a knee ligament and required surgery that, initially at least, jeopardised his £5.5 million move to Lazio. Never a consistent success in Italy, where even in the comeback stages he was under constant pressure to deliver, he nevertheless showed enough flashes to excite.

Gazza's impact on Scottish soccer since joining Glasgow Rangers in 1995 has been immense, even in a multinational team of stars, and he's proved that though his stamina may be suspect, he has lost little of the skill that marked him out as a prospect. He remains a player to build a team around,

as Venables did so successfully at Tottenham: Euro '96, however, will be the testing time, and a failure by Gascoigne to deliver the goods will surely result in his permanent exile under Venables' successor. And that would be a tragedy.

ENGLAND RECORD
(to 31 December 1995)

SEASON	APPS	GOALS
1988-89	5	1
1989-90	12	1
1990-91	3	—
1991-92	—	—
1992-93	7	3
1993-94	2	1
1994-95	3	—
1995-96	3	—
Total	**35**	**6**

PAUL INCE

AGE:	28
BIRTHDATE:	21 OCTOBER 1967
BIRTHPLACE:	ILFORD
HEIGHT:	5' 10"
WEIGHT:	12st 2lb

of the few successes of Manchester United's ill-fated 1994 European Cup campaign and it was little surprise when Arsenal attempted to lure him back to the Premiership in 1996. A club and country combination with David Platt – ironically, also an ex-Manchester United man – would clearly prove attractive to Highbury boss Bruce Rioch and be likely to rekindle Ince's international role.

O ut of sight, out of mind is how £8 million man Paul Ince must have felt when disappearing from the England reckoning following his move to Inter Milan in the summer of 1995. Yet Terry Venables showed faith in the man they call 'the Guv'nor' by reintroducing him to the training squad in January 1996, recognising the fact that after several months of teething troubles the midfield general had recovered his form and most importantly his confidence.

Ince's natural position in front of the back four made him a midfield sweeper, and the role is one he performed to perfection for Manchester United after moving from his first club West Ham in 1989 for £1 million. At that point he had yet to earn international recognition, but Graham Taylor saw him as a replacement for injury-prone club colleague Bryan Robson and Ince happily took on that mantle. His début came in an away game against Spain – the kind of challenge the player relishes – and despite a single-goal loss he maintained his place to play in the remainder of the World Cup campaign (though his unique destructive skills were considered unnecessary against San Marino).

A professionals' professional, he was one

CLUB LEAGUE RECORD
(to start of 1995-96 season)

SEASON	CLUB	APPS	GOALS
1985-86	West Ham Utd	—	—
1986-87	West Ham Utd	10	1
1987-88	West Ham Utd	28	3
1988-89	West Ham Utd	33	3
1989-90	West Ham Utd	1	—
1989-90	Manchester Utd	26	—
1990-91	Manchester Utd	31	3
1991-92	Manchester Utd	33	3
1992-93	Manchester Utd	41	5
1993-94	Manchester Utd	39	8
1994-95	Manchester Utd	36	5
Total		**278**	**31**

ENGLAND RECORD
(to 31 December 1995)

SEASON	APPS	GOALS
1992-93	9	—
1993-94	5	2
1994-95	2	—
1995-96	—	—
Total	**16**	**2**

ROB JONES

AGE:	24
BIRTHDATE:	5 NOVEMBER 1971
BIRTHPLACE:	WREXHAM
HEIGHT:	5' 8"
WEIGHT:	11st

A graduate of the Gresty Road soccer academy run by Crewe's Dario Gradi, Rob Jones was snapped up by Graeme Souness and his form proved to be one of the few bright spots of the Scotsman's Anfield reign. Souness also did the 'Auld Enemy' a favour, for Jones blossomed into an international-class defender, following in the footsteps of his Anfield predecessor Phil Neal for country as well as club. This was fortunate from England's point of view, because Wrexham-born Jones had represented Wales as a schoolboy before 'doing a Ryan Giggs in reverse' and opting to change allegiance while at Youth level.

Just two Under 21 caps followed before Jones was thrown into the international arena against France in 1992 at the age of just 20 and he proved more than mature enough. A powerful overlapper, he set up many Liverpool goals from right-wing crosses, though has no great goalscoring potential in his own right unlike club predecessors Neal and Chris Lawler.

Though Graham Taylor preferred Arsenal's Lee Dixon, Rob Jones became a fixture under Terry Venables, seeing off Paul Parker as his other main rival, but the unstoppable rise of Gary Neville has put a brake on his plans of emulating Phil Neal's half-century of caps. Playing on the left of Liverpool's defensive formation in 1996, he acquitted himself well enough to prove that he is worth his place in England's squad as cover for injured Graeme Le Saux as well as vying for the Number 2 shirt. At 24, Jones still has time on his side.

CLUB LEAGUE RECORD
(to start of 1995-96 season)

SEASON	CLUB	APPS	GOALS
1987-88	Crewe Alex	5	—
1988-89	Crewe Alex	19	1
1989-90	Crewe Alex	11	—
1990-91	Crewe Alex	32	1
1991-92	Crewe Alex	8	—
1991-92	Liverpool	28	—
1992-93	Liverpool	30	—
1993-94	Liverpool	38	—
1994-95	Liverpool	31	—
Total		**202**	**2**

ENGLAND RECORD
(to 31 December 1995)

SEASON	APPS	GOALS
1991-92	1	—
1992-93	—	—
1993-94	3	—
1994-95	4	—
1995-96	—	—
Total	**8**	**—**

ROBERT LEE

AGE:	30
BIRTHDATE:	1 FEBRUARY 1966
BIRTHPLACE:	WEST HAM
HEIGHT:	5' 10"
WEIGHT:	11st 13lb

Lee, dubbed 'the best player in England today' by his club manager (and fellow midfielder) Kevin Keegan, is undoubtedly the mainspring around which the Geordies' Premiership title challenge has been built. And while it was his scoring form of 11 goals in as many games in 1994-95 that forced him into full England contention after just two Under 21 and one B cap, he creates many more openings for others.

Lee's football career began as one of Charlton's many promising youngsters, though he joined on a free from non-league Hornchurch rather than coming up through schoolboy ranks. Born in West Ham, he always wanted to be a Hammer but instead played for the then-groundless Charlton, attracting Newcastle's attention. His £700,000 acquisition in 1992 was a key move in turning a relegation-haunted side into Divisional Champions and the return to the heights they'd last enjoyed in 1989. It wasn't Lee's first experience of the top flight, having played a part in Lennie Lawrence's Houdini years – but transplanting him into a class team worked wonders, and he soon proved the wisdom of Keegan's choice.

Even so, he considered and rejected a move south before blossoming into a world-class performer. Lee made his full début in a 1-1 draw with Romania, scoring England's goal, winning his second cap in the 1-0 defeat of Nigeria. He then played a part in three out of England's last four internationals of 1995, underlining his certain role in Euro '96.

ENGLAND RECORD
(to 31 December 1995)

SEASON	APPS	GOALS
1994-95	2	1
1995-96	3	—
Total	**5**	**1**

CLUB LEAGUE RECORD
(to start of 1995-96 season)

SEASON	CLUB	APPS	GOALS
1983-84	Charlton Ath	11	4
1984-85	Charlton Ath	39	10
1985-86	Charlton Ath	35	8
1986-87	Charlton Ath	33	3
1987-88	Charlton Ath	23	2
1988-89	Charlton Ath	31	5
1989-90	Charlton Ath	37	1
1990-91	Charlton Ath	43	13
1991-92	Charlton Ath	39	12
1992-93	Charlton Ath	7	1
1992-93	Newcastle Utd	36	10
1993-94	Newcastle Utd	41	7
1994-95	Newcastle Utd	35	9
Total		**410**	**85**

STEVE McMANAMAN

AGE:	24
BIRTHDATE:	11 FEBRUARY 1972
BIRTHPLACE:	LIVERPOOL
HEIGHT:	6'
WEIGHT:	10st 6lb

The advantages, resources and facilities available to a club like Liverpool cannot be denied – but the home-grown player faces a special challenge to claim and retain a first-team place in the face of an expectant public and a manager who has the ability to buy a ready-made replacement should the goods not be produced.

Like his club-mate and fellow England hopeful Robbie Fowler, Steve McManaman has bucked the odds to make himself a valued performer for both club and country in a wide right midfield berth. He first came to prominence in Liverpool's 1992 FA Cup campaign that brought Graeme Souness his only honour as Anfield supremo. He recovered from what was a poor season both for himself and the club in 1993-94 to flourish under Roy Evans and push himself from an Under 21 regular (seven caps) to the fringe of the senior squad.

He made his début in late 1994 as substitute for Robert Lee as new England manager Terry Venables shuffled his pack. Further sub appearances in 1995 against Uruguay and Japan illustrated the advantage of having an attacking midfielder on the bench, offering extra options.

His first full game was against Colombia, retaining his place for the next two fixtures and then making yet another appearance as sub against Portugal. There seemed little doubt that Steve McManaman would continue to play a role in Venables' plans, whether for 90 minutes or as fresh legs brought on to torment opposing full-backs and set up chances for Shearer.

ENGLAND RECORD
(to 31 December 1995)

SEASON	APPS	GOALS
1994-95	3	—
1995-96	4	—
Total	**7**	**—**

CLUB LEAGUE RECORD
(to start of 1995-96 season)

SEASON	CLUB	APPS	GOALS
1989-90	Liverpool	—	—
1990-91	Liverpool	2	—
1991-92	Liverpool	30	5
1992-93	Liverpool	31	4
1993-94	Liverpool	30	2
1994-95	Liverpool	40	7
Total		**133**	**18**

GARY NEVILLE

AGE:	21
BIRTHDATE:	18 FEBRUARY 1975
BIRTHPLACE:	BURY
HEIGHT:	5' 11"
WEIGHT:	11st 10lb

Manchester United full-back Gary Neville's rise to fame and international honours had been nothing short of meteoric and, assisted by a timely injury to the man in possession, Rob Jones, he stands in 1996 as first-choice right-back for club and country. So fast was his ascent that just three Under 21 caps preceded his full début.

Older by two years than club colleague and brother Philip, Gary prefers to play as a central defender where his organisation, distribution and tackling make up for a relatively slight stature. He also adds a useful long throw to his team's attacking armoury.

Neville's club début came as substitute in a 1992 UEFA Cup tie against Moscow Torpedo and lasted just two minutes. He played a single game in the 1993-94 Championship season and 18 in the following campaign, so it can be seen he established himself simultaneously for club and country.

His international credentials were first recognised in 1993, when he was one of the England team that took the European title, and just two years later he was taking his full international bow at Wembley against Japan in the 1995 Umbro Cup. Though Warren Barton was preferred the following game, Neville reclaimed his place against Brazil and kept it, despite the return to fitness of Liverpool's Jones – his other main rival for the right-back spot.

Neville's adaptability in filling two positions is likely to ensure him a long and successful run in the full England team.

CLUB LEAGUE RECORD
(to start of 1995-96 season)

SEASON	CLUB	APPS	GOALS
1992-93	Manchester Utd	—	—
1993-94	Manchester Utd	1	—
1994-95	Manchester Utd	18	—
Total		**19**	**—**

ENGLAND RECORD
(to 31 December 1995)

SEASON	APPS	GOALS
1994-95	2	—
1995-96	4	—
Total	**6**	**—**

GARY PALLISTER

AGE:	30
BIRTHDATE:	30 JUNE 1965
BIRTHPLACE:	RAMSGATE
HEIGHT:	6' 4"
WEIGHT:	14st 8lb

An authoritative central defender, Pallister garnered a mantelpiece worth of silverware in his first five seasons at Old Trafford where he forged an impressive partnership with Steve Bruce. Yet he'd already clocked up over 150 games for Middlesbrough whom he joined from non-league Billingham while still a teenager. The £2.3 million fee was considered too high by some, but the player has since proved well worth the price.

International recognition was slow to come under the Robson regime, single games in 1987-88 and 1988-89 against Hungary and Saudi Arabia his only follow-on from nine B appearances. The pace quickened after his transfer, but he had a poor game against Lars Bohinen in a 1993 World Cup qualifier in Olso (where a back three of Adams, Des Walker and Pallister was fielded) and some were surprised Taylor persevered with him.

Club form put him back into contention under Terry Venables, who initially preferred Steve Bould, and the final games of 1995 saw him disputing the place alongside Tony Adams with Newcastle's Steve Howey. A record of one game missed in two seasons (1993-95) attests to both fitness and a calm temperament.

As Old Trafford fans are well aware, Pallister's heading ability has enabled him to pose a real threat at set pieces (though he has yet to open his England account). In international terms, his partnership with Tony Adams might be vulnerable to pace on the ground, but any aerial threat from the likes of Scotland's Duncan Ferguson would certainly be nullified.

CLUB LEAGUE RECORD
(to start of 1995-96 season)

SEASON	CLUB	APPS	GOALS
1984-85	Middlesbrough	—	—
1985-86	Middlesbrough	28	—
1985-86	Darlington (loan)	7	—
1986-87	Middlesbrough	44	1
1987-88	Middlesbrough	44	3
1988-89	Middlesbrough	37	1
1989-90	Middlesbrough	3	—
1989-90	Manchester Utd	35	3
1990-91	Manchester Utd	36	—
1991-92	Manchester Utd	40	1
1992-93	Manchester Utd	42	1
1993-94	Manchester Utd	41	1
1994-95	Manchester Utd	42	2
Total		**399**	**13**

ENGLAND RECORD
(to 31 December 1995)

SEASON	APPS	GOALS
1987-88	1	—
1988-89	1	—
1989-90	—	—
1990-91	2	—
1991-92	1	—
1992-93	4	—
1993-94	4	—
1994-95	5	—
1995-96	2	—
Total	**20**	**—**

STUART PEARCE

AGE:	34
BIRTHDATE:	24 APRIL 1962
BIRTHPLACE:	LONDON
HEIGHT:	5' 10"
WEIGHT:	12st 9lb

Psycho, as he is affectionately nicknamed, has been an England squad regular for a decade now. And if the European Championship in 1996 is to prove his international swansong, the Nottingham Forest defender will be eager to go out on a high note.

In international terms, he'll always be bracketed with Chris Waddle as one of the two England men to fail from the spot in the World Cup semi-final shoot-out in 1990, but this cannot detract from the marvellous service he's rendered under three consecutive managers. And with the sad injury to Graeme Le Saux likely to sideline him for the summer, Pearce's presence is as crucial to England's chances as ever.

Ironically, current Wales boss Bobby Gould was the man who, overlooking Pearce's ability, let the London-born full-back leave Coventry City in 1985 after less than 60 first-team appearances. The error of his ways was apparent as Brian Clough brought the best out of the boy and, after a first cap against Brazil at Wembley in 1987, the £200,000 fee already looked to have lost a final nought.

Since then, Pearce has taken his international caps past the 60 mark, and though his Forest spell has resulted in comparatively little silverware (the League Cup in 1989 and 1990, to date) he continues to supply inspiration as left-back and captain.

His decision to reject a lucrative 1995 deal to finish his career in Japan must have owed something to a desire to play a part in one last England campaign. And should Euro '96 bring up penalties again, it's a fair bet that Stuart Pearce will be the first man to step forward.

CLUB LEAGUE RECORD
(to start of 1995-96 season)

SEASON	CLUB	APPS	GOALS
1983-84	Coventry C	23	—
1984-85	Coventry C	28	4
1985-86	Nott'm Forest	30	1
1986-87	Nott'm Forest	39	6
1987-88	Nott'm Forest	34	5
1988-89	Nott'm Forest	36	6
1989-90	Nott'm Forest	34	5
1990-91	Nott'm Forest	33	11
1991-92	Nott'm Forest	30	5
1992-93	Nott'm Forest	23	2
1993-94	Nott'm Forest	42	6
1994-95	Nott'm Forest	36	8
Total		**388**	**59**

ENGLAND RECORD
(to 31 December 1995)

SEASON	APPS	GOALS
1986-87	2	—
1987-88	3	—
1988-89	10	—
1989-90	15	1
1990-91	11	1
1991-92	9	—
1992-93	3	1
1993-94	3	1
1994-95	3	—
1995-96	3	1
Total	**62**	**5**

DAVID PLATT

AGE:	30
BIRTHDATE:	10 JUNE 1966
BIRTHPLACE:	CHADDERTON
HEIGHT:	5' 10"
WEIGHT:	11st 12lb

Few players have embodied England's hopes in the way David Platt has for much of the 1990s; only Bobby Charlton, Kevin Keegan and Bryan Robson spring to mind. But at the start of 1996 Platt had more in common with Robson than the other two; injury had blighted his return to the English game with Arsenal after a four-season Italian exile, and he was once more on the operating table. England fans with long memories will recall what the absence of Keegan in World Cup '82 and Robson in 1990 meant to their chances – in the latter case, a fit Robson could have made all the difference between success and heroic failure.

Goalscoring midfielder Platt burst on to the scene fully-fledged, it seemed, enjoying an extended international run as his team, Aston Villa, rose to challenge Liverpool for the title – and only just failed. Seven out of eight of his first starts, however, were from the bench.

His retention would have been assured even if club manager Graham Taylor hadn't been selected as the new national manager, thanks to an heroic World Cup campaign in which his single extra-time strike sunk Belgium – thus ending his 'supersub' role. Two more goals were notched against Cameroon (a spectacular header) and Italy, the country in which he'd play most of his future football after one further season with Villa.

His Italian odyssey was the most successful of almost any English player in living memory, transferring clubs within *Serie A* from Bari to Juventus and then Sampdoria before deciding to return to English football for his first taste of the Premiership. Sadly, that was when life started to diverge from the dream script, but a comeback to the colours and an inspirational campaign was not – yet – beyond the realms of reality for a player like Platt.

CLUB LEAGUE RECORD
(to start of 1995-96 season)

SEASON	CLUB	APPS	GOALS
1984-85	Manchester Utd	—	—
1984-85	Crewe Alex	22	5
1985-86	Crewe Alex	43	8
1986-87	Crewe Alex	43	23
1987-88	Crewe Alex	26	19
1987-88	Aston Villa	11	5
1988-89	Aston Villa	38	7
1989-90	Aston Villa	37	19
1990-91	Aston Villa	35	19
1991-92	Bari	29	11
1992-93	Juventus	16	3
1993-94	Sampdoria	29	9
1994-95	Sampdoria	26	8
Total		**355**	**136**

ENGLAND RECORD
(to 31 December 1995)

SEASON	APPS	GOALS
1989-90	11	3
1990-91	11	4
1991-92	10	4
1992-93	10	9
1993-94	6	3
1994-95	7	3
1995-96	—	—
Total	**55**	**26**

DAVID SEAMAN

AGE:	32
BIRTHDATE:	19 SEPTEMBER 1963
BIRTHPLACE:	ROTHERHAM
HEIGHT:	6' 4"
WEIGHT:	14st 10lb

D avid Seaman took the steady and unspectacular route to the top flight and international status – rather like his goalkeeping style, which has always been solid and reliable.

He received his first cap against Saudi Arabia in November 1988 while still at Queens Park Rangers, making the trip across the capital the following year for £1.3 million to displace John Lukic – who, ironically, would return to Leeds, the club where Seaman had been an apprentice but failed to make a first-team appearance.

The next two caps were as substitute for Peter Shilton, Bobby Robson looking towards the World Cup. Robson's successor as manager, Graham Taylor, preferred Chris Woods of Sheffield Wednesday, but Seaman managed to play a part in two European Championship qualifying games in 1991.

A supreme organiser of his club defence at Highbury, Seaman carries his understanding with centre-back Tony Adams through to the national side and together they form a formidable backbone around which to build. Indeed, that was the pairing Terry Venables fashioned his defence round for the last four internationals of 1995, and a defensive record of just two goals conceded suggests he will continue to place his faith in the Highbury duo.

England enter the 1996 European Championship with two vastly experienced international keepers in Seaman and Tim Flowers, rather as the 1970s brought Peter Shilton and Ray Clemence into friendly opposition for the keeper's yellow jersey. Though his rival is younger, the example of Shilton suggests that Seaman will continue in quiet yet confident contention into the next century.

CLUB LEAGUE RECORD
(to start of 1995-96 season)

SEASON	CLUB	APPS	GOALS
1981-82	Leeds Utd	—	—
1982-83	Peterborough Utd	38	—
1983-84	Peterborough Utd	45	—
1984-85	Peterborough Utd	8	—
1984-85	Birmingham C	33	—
1985-86	Birmingham C	42	—
1986-87	QPR	41	—
1987-88	QPR	32	—
1988-89	QPR	35	—
1989-90	QPR	33	—
1990-91	Arsenal	38	—
1991-92	Arsenal	42	—
1992-93	Arsenal	39	—
1993-94	Arsenal	39	—
1994-95	Arsenal	31	—
Total		**496**	**—**

ENGLAND RECORD
(to 31 December 1995)

SEASON	APPS	GOALS
1988-89	2	—
1989-90	1	—
1990-91	4	—
1991-92	2	—
1992-93	—	—
1993-94	5	—
1994-95	3	—
1995-96	4	—
Total	**21**	**—**

ALAN SHEARER

AGE:	25
BIRTHDATE:	13 AUGUST 1970
BIRTHPLACE:	NEWCASTLE
HEIGHT:	6'
WEIGHT:	12st 1lb

To a Scot, Kenny Dalglish, goes the credit of honing the England goalscoring machine that is Alan Shearer. When the ex-Liverpool ace, then manager of Blackburn, signed the player for a record £3.6 million in July 1992 he was already a good striker. Since arriving at Ewood Park from Southampton, he's become a genuinely two-footed, world-class striker for whom the sky's the limit. And all this despite a late-1992 injury, a snapped cruciate ligament, that might have ended the career of someone less determined. His international début was a scoring one, against France in February. Since then, however, his four goals in 20 more games have yet to justify Terry Venables' verdict of 'so good it's frightening'. England have built their formation around him at the top of the Christmas tree, with him as the lone striker with the brief to shield the ball and wait for support.

It's a role not many would relish, especially as it makes the target of criticism when England fail to score, but Shearer takes the knocks of both kinds uncomplainingly. No less an expert than Pelé has written to him expressing 'utmost admiration for the endeavour with which you play the game and the skills you display'.

On the club front, he continues to produce the goods – one goal every 111 minutes in the Premiership in 1994-95. His goals come not just from the six-yard box but in all shapes and sizes. 'If the ball's in the back of the net from half a yard, a yard, or 20 or 30 yards, the buzz is the same.' Could this be the same player ex-Southampton manager Chris Nicholl allegedly claimed 'couldn't trap a bag of cement'?

ENGLAND RECORD
(to 31 December 1995)

SEASON	APPS	GOALS
1991-92	3	1
1992-93	3	1
1993-94	4	1
1994-95	7	2
1995-96	4	—
Total	**21**	**5**

CLUB LEAGUE RECORD
(to start of 1995-96 season)

SEASON	CLUB	APPS	GOALS
1987-88	Southampton	5	3
1988-89	Southampton	10	—
1989-90	Southampton	26	3
1990-91	Southampton	36	4
1991-92	Southampton	41	13
1992-93	Blackburn Rovers	21	16
1993-94	Blackburn Rovers	40	31
1994-95	Blackburn Rovers	42	34
Total		**221**	**104**

TEDDY SHERINGHAM

AGE:	30
BIRTHDATE:	2 APRIL 1966
BIRTHPLACE:	HIGHAMS PARK
HEIGHT:	6'
WEIGHT:	12st 5lb

Teddy Sheringham made his name with Millwall as top scorer with 22 League goals in the Second Division Championship campaign of 1987-88. Having come through the South London club's ranks as an apprentice, he proved a skilful foil to Eire international Tony Cascarino in the target man role and was justifiably voted Player of the Season. He is still Millwall's record scorer.

A move to Nottingham Forest proved a character-building experience, manager Brian Clough – no mean centre-forward himself – taking him under his wing at the City Ground. His departure to White Hart Lane for a £2 million fee left Forest richer...but also relegation material, as Clough admitted in 1993.

Terry Venables, the man who paid the money for Sheringham, has persevered with him since taking the England reins. Graham Taylor had blooded him in important World Cup qualifiers against Poland and Norway, both away games. In the former he ploughed a lone furrow, while Oslo saw him paired with Les Ferdinand.

Since then he's found himself more often than not playing with Alan Shearer, though Venables' Christmas tree formation means a different role from that played at club level alongside Chris Armstrong. A season at Spurs with Jürgen Klinsmann undoubtedly gave many new insights as well as resulting in a combined 52-goal haul, and it will be Sheringham's ability to forge a similar partnership with Shearer that will determine the England team's short-term future.

CLUB LEAGUE RECORD
(to start of 1995-96 season)

SEASON	CLUB	APPS	GOALS
1983-84	Millwall	7	1
1984-85	Millwall	—	—
1984-85	Aldershot (loan)	5	—
1985-86	Millwall	18	4
1986-87	Millwall	42	13
1987-88	Millwall	43	22
1988-89	Millwall	33	11
1989-90	Millwall	31	9
1990-91	Millwall	46	33
1991-92	Nott'm Forest	39	13
1992-93	Nott'm Forest	3	1
1992-93	Tottenham H	38	21
1993-94	Tottenham H	19	14
1994-95	Tottenham H	42	18
Total		**366**	**160**

ENGLAND RECORD
(to 31 December 1995)

SEASON	APPS	GOALS
1992-93	2	—
1993-94	—	—
1994-95	7	1
1995-96	3	1
Total	**12**	**2**

TREVOR SINCLAIR

AGE:	23
BIRTHDATE:	2 MARCH 1973
BIRTHPLACE:	DULWICH
HEIGHT:	5' 10"
WEIGHT:	11st 2lb

ENGLAND RECORD
(to 31 December 1995)

SEASON	APPS	GOALS
–	–	–

London-born left-sided midfielder Trevor Sinclair returned to his capital roots in August 1993 when he joined Queens Park Rangers as replacement for England international Andy Sinton anxious to return north. Blackpool received £750,000 for his services and Rangers had by far the better of the deal – for while injury-jinxed Sinton struggled to maintain his club and international place, Sinclair looked the rising star as Euro '96 dawned.

Rangers had played him up front when injury dictated, but wide midfield is the likely England position for this graduate from the FA School of Excellence. He'll battle Darren Anderton, whose injury gave him the chance to make his Under 21 début in 1993.

His four seasons at Blackpool, including a promotion campaign, gave him a century of League games, whereas had he joined Blackburn, Leeds or either Manchester clubs (all were interested) he would have stayed in reserve. The tutelage of former England midfielder Ray Wilkins has polished the rough diamond to perfection.

A further four Under 21 caps and a five-goal haul were followed by an April 1995 call-up to the senior squad. Should he continue such form – form which is likely to make him a summer target for the Premiership's moneyed élite – Sinclair's distinctive dreadlocks and flamboyant style are likely to become a familiar sight in England teams between now and the next century. And at just 23 as Euro '96 arrives, he can reckon on contesting at least two more such tournaments if form and fitness hold up.

CLUB LEAGUE RECORD
(to start of 1995-96 season)

SEASON	CLUB	APPS	GOALS
1989-90	Blackpool	9	—
1990-91	Blackpool	31	1
1991-92	Blackpool	27	3
1992-93	Blackpool	45	11
1993-94	QPR	32	4
1994-95	QPR	33	4
Total		**177**	**23**

STEVE STONE

AGE:	24
BIRTHDATE:	20 AUGUST 1971
BIRTHPLACE:	GATESHEAD
HEIGHT:	5' 9"
WEIGHT:	11st 3lb

'Three broken legs teaches you not to take anything for granted,' was the comment of Nottingham Forest's Steve Stone after his England début in Oslo in October 1995. He came on in place of Dennis Wise, and settled immediately into the left midfield position in front of club colleague Stuart Pearce as if he'd been there all his life.

The following match at Wembley against Switzerland saw him replace Jamie Redknapp and cap another polished performance by reacting first after an Alan Shearer effort had been saved. Two (half) games, one goal – the scene was set for a full début against Portugal, and he topped this off with England's only goal of the night. A star was born.

If the 24 year old seemed a near-veteran, it wasn't just due to his prematurely thinning thatch. A first-term fixture since 1993, he'd missed just one of Nottingham Forest's League games as the first post-Clough season in the top flight ended with a very creditable third place. And as his England prospects grew, he was gaining European experience for himself as the Midlands club progressed in the UEFA Cup – aided, once again, by Stone's goalscoring knack.

Stone's been likened to another midfield dynamo, Steve Coppell, who believes the newcomer has 'more to his game than just hugging the touchline – and he'll score more goals than I ever did'. Bank on 'Stevie Wonder' playing a part in Euro '96 now he's shaken off his injury-prone past.

CLUB LEAGUE RECORD
(to start of 1995-96 season)

SEASON	CLUB	APPS	GOALS
1989-90	Nott'm Forest	—	—
1990-91	Nott'm Forest	—	—
1991-92	Nott'm Forest	1	—
1992-93	Nott'm Forest	12	1
1993-94	Nott'm Forest	45	5
1994-95	Nott'm Forest	41	5
Total		**99**	**11**

ENGLAND RECORD
(to 31 December 1995)

SEASON	APPS	GOALS
1995-96	3	2
Total	**3**	**2**

IAN WALKER

AGE:	24
BIRTHDATE:	31 OCTOBER 1971
BIRTHPLACE:	WATFORD
HEIGHT:	6' 2"
WEIGHT:	12st 9lb

The son of former Norwich and Everton manager Mike, who was himself a goalkeeper in his playing days, Ian Walker has always attracted the spotlight. Tottenham is his only professional club (though he played three League and League Cup games on loan to Oxford).

Youth, B and nine Under 21 caps made him a clear candidate to accompany senior goalkeepers Seaman and Flowers into European Championship contention. Yet competition has never posed a problem to him, having had to displace Norwegian international keeper Erik Thorstvedt at White Hart Lane. It's never easy for a home-grown player to displace a big-money buy, but the Norwegian appeared just twice in the League and Cups during 1994-95 as Walker's form went from strength to strength under new manager Gerry Francis.

The appointment of former Spurs supremo Terry Venables as national coach clearly didn't hurt his chances either. Well aware of the player's potential, Venables first called him up for the visit to Dublin in February 1995 that resulted in match abandonment. Since then, he's been a part of the national team's plans, though he remains third in the hierarchy behind the two senior keepers, and was an unused substitute against Norway in October 1995.

Having displaced Nigel Martyn, who fell from the international reckoning after Crystal Palace's relegation from the Premiership, Walker has two more rivals in his sights. He missed just one League game for Tottenham in 1994-95, and at 24 clearly aims to make youth pay.

ENGLAND RECORD
(to 31 December 1995)

SEASON	APPS	GOALS
—	—	—

CLUB LEAGUE RECORD
(to start of 1995-96 season)

SEASON	CLUB	APPS	GOALS
1989-90	Tottenham H	—	—
1990-91	Tottenham H	1	—
1990-91	Oxford Utd (loan)	2	—
1990-91	Ipswich T (loan)	—	—
1991-92	Tottenham H	18	—
1992-93	Tottenham H	17	—
1993-94	Tottenham H	11	—
1994-95	Tottenham H	41	—
Total		**90**	**—**

DENNIS WISE

AGE:	29
BIRTHDATE:	15 DECEMBER 1966
BIRTHPLACE:	KENSINGTON
HEIGHT:	5' 6"
WEIGHT:	9st 5lb

Public opinion seems destined forever to be divided on the merits of Dennis Wise as an international player. Critics still tar him with the same rough and ready brush as Wimbledon, with whom he got his first taste of professional football after being released by Southampton. Others point to his temperament, a very public altercation with a taxi-driver that saw him briefly jailed before a successful appeal.

Still more regard the man for whom Chelsea paid £1.6 million in 1990 as simply not up to the task skills-wise. And despite a debut goal against Turkey, two seasons in the international wilderness followed his first England spell.

A renaissance was prompted, however, by tremendous form as Chelsea club captain, and having been recalled by Terry Venables in the early stages of his reign against Romania, Wise ran the subsequent fixture against Nigeria. Statistics suggested that of 50 passes in the latter game, 95 per cent had been accurate. Then came the taxi incident and an injury, but Wise bounced back a second time to play in three out of the four internationals in the winter of 1995.

Wise, a dressing-room favourite, has played over 300 games at the highest level, and certainly seems likely to figure in Euro '96. Yet at 29 he is unlikely to figure in Terry Venables' successor's plans for the next World Cup so will be looking to make the most of every chance he gets.

ENGLAND RECORD
(to 31 December 1995)

SEASON	APPS	GOALS
1990-91	5	1
1991-92	—	—
1992-93	—	—
1993-94	1	—
1994-95	2	—
1995-96	3	—
Total	**11**	**1**

CLUB LEAGUE RECORD
(to start of 1995-96 season)

SEASON	CLUB	APPS	GOALS
1984-85	Wimbledon	1	—
1985-86	Wimbledon	4	—
1986-87	Wimbledon	28	4
1987-88	Wimbledon	30	10
1988-89	Wimbledon	37	5
1989-90	Wimbledon	35	8
1990-91	Chelsea	33	10
1991-92	Chelsea	38	10
1992-93	Chelsea	27	3
1993-94	Chelsea	35	4
1994-95	Chelsea	19	6
Total		**287**	**60**

THE NEARLY MEN
Players on the fringes of Terry Venables' squad

Tottenham wide midfielder Darren Anderton (pictured *below*) has been troubled by injury, but if fit will be a certainty to add to his nine caps under the man who brought him to White Hart Lane from Portsmouth in 1992 for £1.75 million. Blackburn's Graeme Le Saux was unlucky to sustain a leg-break in late 1995 that's likely to rule him out of contesting the left-back slot with Stuart Pearce. Villa's Alan Wright, the man he displaced at Ewood Park, has come along in leaps and bounds and looks a good long-term prospect.

Steve Howey and Gareth Southgate, with three caps between them, are defensive possibilities for the 1998 World Cup, but Euro '96 may prove too soon. Like Southgate, Spurs' as-yet uncapped Sol Campbell can play in defence, but his versatility is likely to keep him a squad player if selected rather than a first-choice.

DARREN ANDERTON

AGE:	24
BIRTHDATE:	3 MARCH 1972
BIRTHPLACE:	SOUTHAMPTON
HEIGHT:	6' 1"
WEIGHT:	12st
ENGLAND CAPS:	9 (3 GOALS)

CLUB LEAGUE RECORD

FROM-TO	CLUB	APPS	GOALS
1990-92	Portsmouth	62	7
1992-95	Spurs	108	17
Total		**170**	**24**

GRAEME LE SAUX

AGE:	27
BIRTHDATE:	17 OCTOBER 1968
BIRTHPLACE:	JERSEY
HEIGHT:	5' 10"
WEIGHT:	11st 4lb
ENGLAND CAPS:	12 (1 GOAL)

CLUB LEAGUE RECORD

FROM-TO	CLUB	APPS	GOALS
1987-93	Chelsea	90	8
1993-95	Blackburn R	89	5
Total		**179**	**13**

ALAN WRIGHT

AGE:	24
BIRTHDATE:	28 SEPTEMBER 1971
BIRTHPLACE:	ASHTON-UNDER-LYME
HEIGHT:	5' 4"
WEIGHT:	9st 4lb
ENGLAND CAPS:	—

CLUB LEAGUE RECORD

FROM-TO	CLUB	APPS	GOALS
1989-91	Blackpool	98	—
1991-94	Blackburn R	74	1
1994-95	Aston Villa	8	—
Total		**180**	**1**

STEVE HOWEY

AGE:	24
BIRTHDATE:	26 OCTOBER 1971
BIRTHPLACE:	SUNDERLAND
HEIGHT:	6' 1"
WEIGHT:	10st 5lb
ENGLAND CAPS: 3	

CLUB LEAGUE RECORD

FROM-TO	CLUB	APPS	GOALS
1989-95	Newcastle Utd	118	4

GARETH SOUTHGATE

AGE:	25
BIRTHDATE:	3 SEPTEMBER 1970
BIRTHPLACE:	WATFORD
HEIGHT:	5' 10"
WEIGHT:	12st 3lb
ENGLAND CAPS: 1	

CLUB LEAGUE RECORD

FROM-TO	CLUB	APPS	GOALS
1989-95	Crystal Palace	152	15

SOL CAMPBELL

AGE:	21
BIRTHDATE:	18 SEPTEMBER 1974
BIRTHPLACE:	NEWHAM
HEIGHT:	6' 2"
WEIGHT:	14st 1lb
ENGLAND CAPS: —	

CLUB LEAGUE RECORD

FROM-TO	CLUB	APPS	GOALS
1992-95	Spurs	65	1

ROBBIE FOWLER

AGE:	21
BIRTHDATE:	9 APRIL 1975
BIRTHPLACE:	LIVERPOOL
HEIGHT:	5' 11"
WEIGHT:	11st 10lb
ENGLAND CAPS: —	

CLUB LEAGUE RECORD

FROM-TO	CLUB	APPS	GOALS
1992-95	Liverpool	70	37

JAMIE REDKNAPP

AGE:	23
BIRTHDATE:	25 JUNE 1973
BIRTHPLACE:	BARTON ON SEA
HEIGHT:	6'
WEIGHT:	12st
ENGLAND CAPS: 3	

CLUB LEAGUE RECORD

FROM-TO	CLUB	APPS	GOALS
1990-91	Bournemouth	13	—
1991-95	Liverpool	111	10
Total		**124**	**10**

The Liverpool duo of Robbie Fowler (*above right*) and Jamie Redknapp are near certainties for the '98 World Cup squad, but competition this time may shade them out of the final 22. They are the youthful counterparts of Arsenal's Paul Merson (14 caps) and Ian Wright (20), both of whom seem to have missed the international boat.

Above: Paul Merson in World Cup action against Norway in October 1992.

Record striker Andy Cole still has only one substitute's appearance against Uruguay in 1995 to his name, but if he finally produces his Newcastle form at Old Trafford could still prove impossible to ignore: he's only 24. But the man who must be hoping to catch the eye of Terry Venables' successor is Southampton's Matt Le Tissier – last seen in an England shirt in the abandoned Dublin game in early 1995.

If six caps is the sum total of his recognition, he'll join Marsh, Currie, Worthington and Bowles, flair players of yesteryear, in sharing the unwanted label: 'the men England forgot'.

PAUL MERSON

AGE:	28
BIRTHDATE:	20 MARCH 1968
BIRTHPLACE:	LONDON
HEIGHT:	6'
WEIGHT:	13st 2lb
ENGLAND CAPS:	14

CLUB LEAGUE RECORD

FROM-TO	CLUB	APPS	GOALS
1985-95	Arsenal	257	67
1987	Brentford (loan)	7	—
Total		**264**	**67**

MATT LE TISSIER

AGE:	27
BIRTHDATE:	14 OCTOBER 1968
BIRTHPLACE:	GUERNSEY
HEIGHT:	6' 1"
WEIGHT:	13st 8lb
ENGLAND CAPS:	6

CLUB LEAGUE RECORD

FROM-TO	CLUB	APPS	GOALS
1986-95	Southampton	292	119

IAN WRIGHT

AGE:	32
BIRTHDATE:	3 NOVEMBER 1963
BIRTHPLACE:	WOOLWICH
HEIGHT:	5' 9"
WEIGHT:	11st 8lb
ENGLAND CAPS:	20 (5 GOALS)

CLUB LEAGUE RECORD

FROM-TO	CLUB	APPS	GOALS
1985-91	Crystal Palace	225	89
1991-95	Arsenal	131	80
Total		**356**	**169**

ANDY COLE

AGE:	24
BIRTHDATE:	15 OCTOBER 1971
BIRTHPLACE:	NOTTINGHAM
HEIGHT:	5' 11"
WEIGHT:	11st 2lb
ENGLAND CAPS:	1

CLUB LEAGUE RECORD

FROM-TO	CLUB	APPS	GOALS
1989-92	Arsenal	1	—
1991	Fulham (loan)	13	3
1992	Bristol C (loan)	12	8
1992-93	Bristol C	29	12
1993-95	Newcastle Utd	70	55
1995	Man Utd	18	12
Total		**143**	**90**

6: ENGLAND LANDMARKS

A century of England football has seen many records broken, anniversaries celebrated and personal bests established

ENGLAND INTERNATIONAL FIRSTS

The first substitute to be used by England was Jimmy Mullen in England's 4-1 victory in Belgium in May 1950. He also became the first sub to score after finding the net shortly after the interval.

Stan Mortensen scored England's **first ever goal in the World Cup Finals** when he headed home against Chile in June 1950 in Brazil's Maracana Stadium.

Billy Wright became the **first England player to register 100 appearances** for his country in April 1959. The assembled crowd waiting to watch the match against Scotland gave him a standing ovation as he led his team on to the pitch. His 105th and last match was against the USA the following month in Los Angeles.

England's **first European Nations Cup match** was against France in Sheffield on 3 October 1962. A dubious penalty decision by Danish referee Hansen gave Ron Flowers (pictured *above*) the opportunity to bring England level after Goujon had given the visitors the lead, and the match finished all square.

Alan Mullery gained the unwanted distinction of becoming the **first England player to be sent off** in a full international in June 1968 when dismissed during a European Nations Cup match against Yugoslavia in Italy. The next such departure was five years later, when Alan Ball was sent for an early bath in a World Cup qualifying match in Poland.

Geoff Hurst's three-goal haul at Wembley in July 1966 was the **first hat-trick ever scored in a World Cup Final.** It remains so today, three decades later. The West Ham striker's tournament total was an astounding four goals in three games, Jimmy Greaves having played in the first three group games.

Viv Anderson of Nottingham Forest, now assistant manager of Middlesbrough, became the **first coloured player** to pull on an England shirt when he made his début against Czechoslovakia in November 1978. England won 1-0 with a goal from Steve Coppell.

The 2-1 win over Yugoslavia at Wembley on 13 December 1989 saw England use **five substitutes in a match** for the first time. Dave Beasant (replacing Peter Shilton), Tony Dorigo (Stuart Pearce), David Platt (Michael Thomas), Steve McMahon (Bryan Robson) and Steve Hodge (David Rocastle) were the players whose names went down in history.

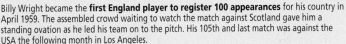

The **first Third Division player** to be capped by England was Millwall's Jack Fort, who played in the 2-0 victory over Belgium on 21 May 1921. 18 more have since attained the honour, the most recent being Steve Bull, of Wolves, against Scotland in May 1989.

England's **first penalty shoot-out** took place against West Germany in the semi-final of the 1990 World Cup in Italy. With the scores level at 1-1 after extra time, following second-half goals from Brehme and Lineker (pictured *right*), it was up to the

ENGLAND INTERNATIONAL FIRSTS cont'd.

five spot-kickers and both keepers to decide who would face Argentina in the Final.

Lineker, Beardsley and Platt scored for England, while Brehme, Matthäus and Riedle replied for the Germans. Stuart Pearce then saw his shot saved, and after Thon had put his side 4-3 up it was down to Chris Waddle to keep England in the competition. His kick went over the bar and England failed to make it to their second Final.

Above: Jimmy Greaves scored three or more goals for England on six different occasions.

POSTWAR HAT-TRICKS OR BETTER

A hat-trick in a competitive game is always special – but the ability to perform the feat in an England shirt is granted to few.

PLAYER	SCORED		OPPONENTS	HOME/AWAY	RESULT
Roy Bentley					
10 November 1954	3	v	Wales	(H)	3-2
Luther Blissett					
13 October 1982	3	v	Luxembourg	(H)	9-0
John Byrne					
17 May 1964	3	v	Portugal	(A)	4-3
Bobby Charlton					
28 May 1959	3	v	USA	(A)	8-1
19 October 1960	3	v	Luxembourg	(A)	9-0
10 May 1961	3	v	Mexico	(H)	8-0
5 June 1963	3	v	Switzerland	(A)	8-1
Tom Finney					
14 May 1950	4	v	Portugal	(A)	5-3
Jimmy Greaves					
19 October 1960	3	v	Luxembourg	(A)	9-0
15 April 1961	3	v	Scotland	(H)	9-3
20 May 1962	3	v	Peru	(A)	4-0
20 November 1963	4	v	Northern Ireland	(H)	8-3
3 October 1964	3	v	Northern Ireland	(A)	4-3
29 June 1966	4	v	Norway	(A)	6-1
Johnny Haynes					
22 October 1958	3	v	USSR	(H)	5-0
Roger Hunt					
27 May 1964	4	v	USA	(A)	10-0
Geoff Hurst					
30 July 1966	3	v	West Germany	(H)	4-2
12 March 1969	3	v	France	(H)	5-0
Tommy Lawton					
27 November 1946	4	v	Holland	(H)	8-2
27 May 1947	4	v	Portugal	(A)	10-0

Left: Gary Lineker scores in the 1990 World Cup semi-final.

Above: Ian Wright, scorer of four against San Marino in November 1993.

PLAYER	SCORED		OPPONENTS	HOME/AWAY	RESULT
Gary Lineker					
16 October 1985	3	v	Turkey	(H)	5-0
11 June 1986	3	v	Poland	(A)	3-0
18 February 1987	4	v	Spain	(A)	4-2
14 October 1987	3	v	Turkey	(H)	8-0
12 June 1991	4	v	Malaysia	(A)	4-2
Malcolm Macdonald					
16 April 1975	5	v	Cyprus	(H)	5-0
Wilf Mannion					
28 September 1946	3	v	Northern Ireland	(A)	7-2
Jackie Milburn					
15 October 1949	3	v	Wales	(A)	4-1
Stan Mortensen					
27 May 1947	4	v	Portugal	(A)	10-0
19 November 1947	3	v	Sweden	(H)	4-2
9 October 1948	3	v	Northern Ireland	(A)	6-2
Terry Paine					
20 November 1963	3	v	Northern Ireland	(H)	8-3
Fred Pickering					
27 May 1964	3	v	USA	(H)	10-0
David Platt					
17 February 1993	4	v	San Marino	(H)	6-0
Bryan Robson					
14 November 1984	3	v	Turkey	(A)	8-0
John Rowley					
16 November 1949	4	v	Northern Ireland	(H)	9-2
Tommy Taylor					
5 December 1956	3	v	Denmark	(H)	5-2
8 May 1957	3	v	Eire	(H)	5-1
Dennis Wilshaw					
2 April 1955	4	v	Scotland	(H)	7-2
Ian Wright					
17 November 1993	4	v	San Marino	(A)	7-1

TOP 20 GOALSCORERS

No one player has yet scored a half-century of goals for England – and, given the intensity of the modern game, it looks less and less likely as time passes. Gary Lineker was still in with a shout of at least equalling Bobby Charlton's record before Graham Taylor controversially withdrew him from his final match against Sweden – an act that cost him more public sympathy than anything else in his reign.

In terms of strike rate, dividing goals scored by games played, the leaders of the pack are George Camsell, Vivian Woodward, Steve Bloomer and Dixie Dean. It should be remembered, though, that substitute appearances are included as full games in these totals, and David Platt gained seven out of his first eight caps coming from the bench.

	PLAYER	CAREER DATES	TOTAL	GAMES PLD	STRIKE RATE
1	Bobby Charlton	1958-70	49	106	0.46
2	Gary Lineker	1984-92	48	80	0.60
3	Jimmy Greaves	1959-67	44	57	0.77
4	Tom Finney	1946-58	30	76	0.39
4	Nat Lofthouse	1950-58	30	33	0.91
6	Vivian Woodward	1903-11	29	23	1.26
7	Steve Bloomer	1895-1907	28	23	1.22
8	David Platt	1989-	26	55	0.47
8	Bryan Robson	1980-91	26	90	0.29
10	Geoff Hurst	1966-72	24	49	0.49
11	Stan Mortensen	1947-53	23	25	0.92
12	Tommy Lawton	1939-48	22	23	0.96
13	Mick Channon	1972-77	21	46	0.46
13	Kevin Keegan	1972-82	21	63	0.33
15	Martin Peters	1966-74	20	67	0.30
16	George Camsell	1929-36	18	9	2.00
16	Dixie Dean	1927-33	18	16	1.13
16	Johnny Haynes	1954-62	18	56	0.32
16	Roger Hunt	1962-69	18	34	0.53
20	Tommy Taylor	1953-57	16	19	0.84
20	Tony Woodcock	1978-86	16	42	0.38

Above: England's record goalscorer with 49, Bobby Charlton.

Right: David Platt's tally of 26 is impressive for a midfielder.

Left: Kenny Sansom, sixth in the appearances list with 86, played most of his League football with Crystal Palace, Arsenal, QPR and Coventry.

Below: Though he retired from international football after the 1990 World Cup, Peter Shilton was still active in the Premier League in the 1995-96 season.

TOP 20 APPEARANCES

As with League football, Peter Shilton takes the top spot – though a rivalry with Ray Clemence, who gained 61 caps between 1972 and 1983, cost Shilton (born 1949) the chance to stake an even more commanding lead. He was 21 when awarded his first full cap against East Germany, 40 when he won his last. And in 1996 he was still active at the highest club level with West Ham.

Captain Billy Wright's proud record stood for 11 years. With Stuart Pearce, now in his 30s, the only currently active player in the listings, Shilton's tenure will undoubtedly last longer.

1	Peter Shilton	1970-90	125
2	Bobby Moore	1962-73	108
3	Bobby Charlton	1958-70	106
4	Billy Wright	1946-59	105
5	Bryan Robson	1980-91	90
6	Kenny Sansom	1979-88	86
7	Ray Wilkins	1976-86	84
8	Gary Lineker	1984-92	80
9	John Barnes	1983-95	79
10	Terry Butcher	1980-90	77
11	Tom Finney	1946-58	76
12	Gordon Banks	1963-72	73
13	Alan Ball	1965-75	72
14	Martin Peters	1966-74	67
15	Dave Watson	1974-82	65
16	Kevin Keegan	1972-82	63
16	Ray Wilson	1960-68	63
18	Emlyn Hughes	1969-80	62
18	Stuart Pearce	1987-	62
18	Chris Waddle	1985-91	62

POST WORLD WAR 2 ONE-CAP WONDERS

It's unusual for a player to earn international recognition only to win a single, solitary cap, particularly since the selection committee system was abolished.

Seven débutants were blooded against Northern Ireland by Walter Winterbottom after England failed to progress in the 1954 World Cup, but a poor overall performance saw only three retained.

Dave Pegg of Manchester United was one of the Busby Babes to lose his life at Munich, while Tony Kay's career was cut short by match-fixing allegations.

Manchester United keeper Alex Stepney was blooded just before a European Nations Final, but remained third choice behind Banks and Bonetti. Had injury required him to step up, manager Ramsey knew he had at least been tried at international level.

Many more were unfortunate enough to be understudying one or more England regulars, and waited in vain for injury or inconsistency to give them another chance. Goalkeepers, of course, had less chance than most, and it's surprising that just five of those named below – marked with an asterisk – are custodians.

The stigma of achieving only one cap didn't necessarily harm players' confidence. Manchester United's Bill Foulkes, discarded in 1954, went on to win a European Cup medal 14 years later, while West Brom's Tony Brown was the club's record goalscorer, outstripping club-mate Jeff Astle who gained five times as many caps. Others, like Nicholson, Hollins and Perryman, went into management.

Of the 1990s contenders for this unwanted title of one-cap wonders, Cole, Unsworth and Southgate are all young and talented enough to gain further recognition.

PLAYER	(TEAM)	DATE		OPPONENTS	RESULT	GOALS
Jimmy Hagan	(Sheff Utd)	26 September 1948	v	Denmark	0-0	
Jack Haines	(West Brom)	1 December 1948	v	Switzerland	6-0	2
Eddie Shimwell	(Blackpool)	13 May 1949	v	Sweden	1-3	
Jesse Pye	(Wolves)	21 September 1949	v	Eire	0-2	
Bernard Streten*	(Luton T)	16 November 1949	v	N Ireland	9-2	
Jackie Lee	(Derby Co)	7 October 1950	v	N Ireland	4-1	1
Bill Nicholson	(Spurs)	19 May 1951	v	Portugal	5-2	1
Arthur Willis	(Spurs)	3 October 1951	v	France	2-2	
Arthur Milton	(Arsenal)	28 November 1951	v	Austria	2-2	
Derek Ufton	(Charlton Ath)	21 October 1953	v	Rest of Europe	4-4	
Stan Rickaby	(West Brom)	11 November 1953	v	N Ireland	3-1	
George Robb	(Spurs)	25 November 1953	v	Hungary	3-6	
Ernie Taylor	(Blackpool)	25 November 1953	v	Hungary	3-6	
Harry Clarke	(Spurs)	3 April 1954	v	Scotland	4-2	
Ray Barlow	(West Brom)	2 October 1954	v	N Ireland	2-0	
Bill Foulkes	(Man Utd)	2 October 1954	v	N Ireland	2-0	
Brian Pilkington	(Burnley)	2 October 1954	v	N Ireland	2-0	
John Wheeler	(Bolton W)	2 October 1954	v	N Ireland	2-0	
Ken Armstrong	(Chelsea)	2 April 1955	v	Scotland	7-2	
Jimmy Meadows	(Man C)	2 April 1955	v	Scotland	7-2	
Geoff Bradford	(Bristol R)	2 October 1955	v	Denmark	5-1	1
David Pegg	(Man Utd)	19 May 1957	v	Eire	1-1	
Danny Clapton	(Aston Villa)	26 November 1958	v	Wales	2-2	
Ken Brown	(West Ham Utd)	18 November 1959	v	N Ireland	2-1	
John Angus	(Burnley)	27 May 1961	v	Austria	1-3	

Above: Manchester United's Andy Cole had earned just one England cap by the end of 1995. The public clamoured for his inclusion in the national team after his goalscoring exploits at Newcastle but their prayers went unanswered for a long time, though it is certain that he will add to his appearance against Uruguay.

PLAYER	(TEAM)	DATE		OPPONENTS	RESULT	GOALS
Brian Miller	(Burnley)	27 May 1961	v	Austria	1-3	
John Fantham	(Sheff Wed)	28 September 1961	v	Luxembourg	4-1	
Ray Charnley	(Sheff Wed)	3 October 1962	v	France	1-1	
Chris Crowe	(Wolves)	3 October 1962	v	France	1-1	
Ron Henry	(Spurs)	27 February 1963	v	France	2-5	
Ken Shellito	(Chelsea)	29 May 1963	v	Czechoslovakia	4-2	
Tony Kay	(Everton)	5 June 1963	v	Switzerland	8-1	1
Gerry Young	(Sheff Wed)	18 November 1964	v	Wales	2-1	
Derek Temple	(Everton)	12 May 1965	v	W Germany	1-0	
Gordon Harris	(Burnley)	5 January 1966	v	Poland	1-1	
John Hollins	(Chelsea)	24 May 1967	v	Spain	2-0	
Alex Stepney*	(Man Utd)	22 May 1968	v	Sweden	3-1	
Ian Storey-Moore	(Nott'm Forest)	14 January 1970	v	Holland	0-0	
Colin Harvey	(Everton)	3 February 1971	v	Malta	1-0	
Tony Brown	(West Brom)	19 May 1971	v	Wales	0-0	
Tommy Smith	(Liverpool)	19 May 1971	v	Wales	0-0	
Jeff Blockley	(Arsenal)	11 October 1972	v	Yugoslavia	1-1	
John Richards	(Wolves)	12 May 1973	v	N Ireland	2-1	
Phil Parkes*	(QPR)	3 April 1974	v	Portugal	0-0	
Brian Little	(Aston Villa)	21 May 1975	v	Wales	2-2	
Phil Boyer	(Norwich C)	24 March 1976	v	Wales	2-1	
Jimmy Rimmer*	(Arsenal)	28 May 1976	v	Italy	3-2	
Charlie George	(Derby Co)	8 September 1976	v	Eire	1-1	
John Gidman	(Aston Villa)	30 March 1977	v	Luxembourg	5-0	
Trevor Whymark	(Ipswich T)	12 October 1977	v	Luxembourg	2-0	
Alan Sunderland	(Arsenal)	31 May 1980	v	Australia	2-1	
Peter Ward	(Brighton)	31 May 1980	v	Australia	2-1	
Paul Goddard	(West Ham Utd)	2 June 1982	v	Iceland	1-1	1
Steve Perryman	(Spurs)	2 June 1982	v	Iceland	1-1	
Nick Pickering	(Sunderland)	19 June 1983	v	Australia	1-1	
Nigel Spink*	(Aston Villa)	19 June 1983	v	Australia	1-1	
Brian Stein	(Luton T)	29 February 1984	v	France	0-2	
Peter Davenport	(Nott'm Forest)	25 March 1985	v	Eire	2-1	
Danny Wallace	(Southampton)	29 January 1986	v	Egypt	4-0	1
Brian Marwood	(Arsenal)	16 November 1988	v	Saudi Arabia	1-1	
Mel Sterland	(Sheff Wed)	16 November 1988	v	Saudi Arabia	1-1	
Mike Phelan	(Man Utd)	15 November 1989	v	Italy	0-0	
Mark Walters	(Rangers)	3 June 1991	v	New Zealand	1-0	
Andy Gray	(C Palace)	13 November 1991	v	Poland	1-1	
David White	(Man C)	9 September 1992	v	Spain	0-1	
Andy Cole	(Man Utd)	29 March 1995	v	Uruguay	0-0	
David Unsworth	(Everton)	3 June 1995	v	Japan	2-1	
Gareth Southgate	(Aston Villa)	12 December 1995	v	Portugal	1-1	

SCORED ON THEIR POSTWAR DÉBUT
(PLAYERS EARNING MORE THAN ONE CAP)

The first postwar international against Northern Ireland saw nine players make their England débuts – so with seven goals scored a hat-trick of first-time marksmen seems about right.

Liverpool's Chris Lawler is worth singling out, because he played at right-back and wasn't selected for his scoring prowess; his goal was a 35-yarder, no less. The list also contains two future England managers in Bobby Robson and Don Revie.

Tom Finney	28 September 1946	1	v	N Ireland	(A)	7-2
Bobby Langton	28 September 1946	1	v	N Ireland	(A)	7-2
Wilf Mannion	28 September 1946	3	v	N Ireland	(A)	7-2
Stan Mortensen	27 May 1947	4	v	Portugal	(A)	10-0
Jackie Milburn	9 October 1948	1	v	N Ireland	(A)	6-2
Johnny Hancocks	2 December 1948	2	v	Switzerland	(H)	6-0
Jack Rowley	2 December 1948	2	v	Switzerland	(H)	6-0

Left: Fulham's one-club man Johnny Haynes started his England career on the right foot when he scored on his début against Northern Ireland in October 1954. Don Revie, another débutant in that match, scored the other.

Above: Gerry Hitchens notched his début goal in the 8-0 Wembley thrashing of Mexico in 1961.

Above: Dennis Wise scores the only goal of the game in the European Championship qualifier away to Turkey in 1991.

Johnny Morris	18 May 1949	1	v	Norway	(A)	4-1
Jack Froggatt	16 November 1949	1	v	N Ireland	(H)	9-2
Nat Lofthouse	22 November 1950	2	v	Yugoslavia	(H)	2-2
Harold Hassall	14 April 1951	1	v	Scotland	(H)	2-3
Dennis Wilshaw	10 October 1953	2	v	Wales	(A)	4-1
Johnny Nicholls	3 April 1954	1	v	Scotland	(A)	4-2
Johnny Haynes	2 October 1954	1	v	N Ireland	(A)	2-0
Don Revie	2 October 1954	1	v	N Ireland	(A)	2-0
John Atyeo	30 November 1955	1	v	Spain	(H)	4-1
Colin Grainger	9 May 1956	2	v	Brazil	(H)	4-2
Gordon Astall	20 May 1956	1	v	Finland	(A)	5-1
Johnny Brooks	14 November 1956	1	v	Wales	(H)	3-1
Derek Kevan	6 April 1957	1	v	Scotland	(H)	2-1
Alan A'Court	6 November 1957	1	v	N Ireland	(H)	2-3
Bobby Robson	27 November 1957	2	v	France	(H)	4-0
Bobby Charlton	19 April 1958	1	v	Scotland	(A)	4-0
Warren Bradley	6 May 1959	1	v	Italy	(H)	2-2
Jimmy Greaves	17 May 1959	1	v	Peru	(A)	1-4
Joe Baker	18 November 1959	1	v	N Ireland	(H)	2-1
Ray Parry	18 November 1959	1	v	N Ireland	(H)	2-1
Bobby Smith	8 October 1960	1	v	N Ireland	(A)	5-2
Gerry Hitchens	10 May 1961	1	v	Mexico	(H)	8-0
Ray Pointer	28 September 1961	1	v	Luxembourg	(H)	4-1
Roger Hunt	4 April 1962	1	v	Austria	(H)	3-1
Mike O'Grady	20 October 1962	2	v	N Ireland	(A)	3-1

Fred Pickering	27 May 1964	3	v	USA	(A)	10-0
Frank Wignall	18 November 1964	2	v	Wales	(H)	2-1
Allan Clarke	11 June 1970	1	v	Czechoslovakia	(A)	1-0
Chris Lawler	12 May 1971	1	v	Malta	(H)	5-0
David Johnson	21 May 1975	2	v	Wales	(H)	2-2
Ray Kennedy	24 March 1976	1	v	Wales	(A)	2-1
Peter Taylor	24 March 1976	1	v	Wales	(A)	2-1
Glenn Hoddle	22 November 1979	1	v	Bulgaria	(H)	2-0
Sammy Lee	17 November 1982	1	v	Greece	(A)	3-0
Mark Chamberlain	15 December 1982	1	v	Luxembourg	(H)	9-0
Steve Bull	27 May 1989	1	v	Scotland	(A)	2-0
Dennis Wise	1 May 1991	1	v	Turkey	(A)	1-0
Alan Shearer	19 February 1992	1	v	France	(H)	2-0
Les Ferdinand	17 February 1993	1	v	San Marino	(H)	6-0
Robert Lee	12 October 1994	1	v	Romania	(H)	1-1

ANNIVERSARIES AND FAREWELLS

The 75th anniversary of the English Football Association was celebrated by a match between England and a FIFA Rest of Europe team at Wembley on 21 October 1953. Mortensen, Mullen 2 and Ramsey (*pen*) scored for the home side in a 4-4 draw.

Nottingham Forest's Neil Webb become the 1,000th player to be used in a England international when he came on as substitute for Glenn Hoddle during the 3-1 defeat away to West Germany on 9 September 1987.

Below: Neil Webb, pictured *(on the floor)* scoring against Hungary in 1992, holds the honour of being the 1,000th player used in an England international.

15 May 1957 saw Stanley Matthews' last England appearance in the 4-1 victory over Denmark. At the age of 42, his international career was coming to an end after 54 appearances and three goals. Matthews continued to play in the domestic game with Stoke, however, until 6 February 1965. He celebrated his 50th birthday five days earlier – and more recognition was awarded him when he became the first footballer to be knighted in the New Year's honours list.

The England-Scotland fixture thrown up by the Euro '96 draw was the one that attracted most publicity. And that wasn't surprising, since fixtures against Scotland have something of a history behind them. The first accounted for England's first ever international on 30 November 1872 – a goalless draw – and the 100th official international was on 29 May 1982, this time a 1-0 England win.

Two years later the fixture at Hampden on 26 May 1984 brought to an end the Home International Championships, though the single fixture would continue until 1989. At that stage, the record read: England 43, Scotland 40, drawn 24.

Left: The programme from the Hampden Park clash in 1980, four years before the Home Internationals ceased. England won 2-0.

Right: The mercurial Stanley Matthews, whose England career began in 1935 against Wales.

ENGLAND RECORD BREAKERS

In the 66th meeting between England and Northern Ireland, Tom Finney of Preston established a new scoring record. His goal in the October 1958 clash took his England tally to 30. His sole claim to this title would last just one match, however, as Bolton's Nat Lofthouse registered his 30th successful strike in the following game against USSR.

The Home International against Wales saw Bobby Charlton register his 31st goal for England, thus overtaking both Finney and Lofthouse's hauls. He would go on to record a so-far unbeaten total of 49 goals (in a new record 106 appearances) before his international retirement in June 1970. While Gary Lineker made an impressive effort in the 1980s and 1990s to claim the mantle of his country's top scorer, he would ultimately have to settle for second place on 48 (in 80 games).

Bobby Moore set a new appearance record of 108 caps on 14 November 1973, beating Bobby Charlton by two. Moore's record would stand until June 1989, when Peter Shilton overtook him on his way to 125.

Newcastle's Malcolm Macdonald (pictured *above*) equalled the scoring record for an individual in a match with a five-goal haul against Cyprus on 16 April 1975 at Wembley. His tally placed him alongside Howard Vaughton (1882), Steve Bloomer (1896), Gilbert Smith (1899) and Willie Hall, (pictured *left*, 1938) as the only players ever to have scored five in a game.

The 4-3 defeat away to Austria in June 1979 was the first time that England had conceded more than three goals since Brazil triumphed in Rio in May 1964.

England suffered their heaviest international defeat when they lost 7-1 to Hungary in the Nep Stadium, Budapest on 23 May 1954. Newcastle United's Ivor Broadis netted the consolation goal.

YOUNGEST AND OLDEST

YOUNGEST PREWAR:					
James Prinsep	(Clapham Rovers)	5 April 1879	v	Scotland	17 yrs 252 days

YOUNGEST POSTWAR:					
Duncan Edwards	(Man Utd)	2 April 1955	v	Scotland	18 yrs 183 days

OLDEST DÉBUTANT
Leslie Compton (Arsenal) was the oldest player to make his England début at 38 years and 2 months when he played against Wales in November 1950.

Right: Bobby Moore, the man who lifted the World Cup at Wembley and whose record of 108 appearances stood for 16 years.

ON PLAYING FOR ENGLAND

'I'll never forget the faces of the two Spanish full-backs when facing 4-4-2 for the first time. We had no winger so they just stood in space while we all piled up the middle.'
Bobby Charlton, on beating Spain 2-0 in Madrid in December 1965

'I always enjoyed playing against Brazil the most because they were so individually talented – and the best.'
Bobby Moore

'As I sat in the dressing room I could hear the great crowd singing as only Welsh folk can sing, and I must admit to being nervous beyond description. Then Eddie Hapgood, our skipper, came over to me, patted me on the shoulder, and said, "Good luck, Tom. Oh!. And by the way, you'll take any penalties we get."
  'So here I was in my first international match and entrusted with the penalty kicks. A good job I was, too, or else I might never have kicked the ball, for Tommy Jones (Wales' centre-half) played a blinder, and the only real shot I got was when we were awarded a second-half penalty from which I scored.'
Tommy Lawton, on his début in the 4-2 defeat away to Wales in October 1938 as told in his autobiography *My Twenty Years Of Soccer*

'I shall always remember that goal against Belgium, for I regard it as the best I've ever scored with my head. Long before the ball came to me I had a hunch I was going to score. Tommy Taylor, our inside-left, was the architect, for he made ground with the ball and then pushed an accurate pass to Tom Finney. In his own inimitable way the England left-winger strolled round right-back Dries, and to many appeared certain to run the ball out of play. Some second sense, however, told me the ball was going to be crossed by Tom. Sure enough it was, a few inches off the ground. I cannot explain why I tried a header instead of a drive, but I threw myself at the ball, my forehead connected in copybook fashion, and on all fours I watched it pass just inside the right-hand post.'
Nat Lofthouse, on England's 4-4 draw against Belgium in the 1954 World Cup as told in his autobiography *Goals Galore*

Left: Though he never registered a hat-trick for England, Nat Lofthouse came close on 12 occasions by scoring a brace of international goals.

ON PLAYING FOR ENGLAND

'A very proud moment for me and a lifetime ambition realised. Mind you, but for the Munich accident I certainly wouldn't have been picked.'
Bobby Charlton, on his England début against Scotland in April 1958

'Bryan Robson's goal after 27 seconds was the best England goal I remember. Steve Coppell's long throw hit my head, dropping for Bryan to score. It was such a feeling, all the hard work prior felt worth it.'
Terry Butcher, on England's record start to the 1982 World Cup match against France in Bilbao

'When Billy (Wright), for the first time, led the England team on to the field at Belfast, he was experiencing the proudest moment of his life. I, too, feel proud to think that I was one of the fellows who walked with him that sunny October afternoon.
   To make my début for England in the same forward line as Stanley Matthews was in itself a great moment in my career. Stanley later made it a lifelong memory with as wonderful a performance as ever you'll see in a football match. Stanley was at his brilliant and bewildering best. The Irish defence just didn't know what to make of him, and it was with a good deal of satisfaction I made the pass to him which he used to score England's first goal. Then Stan Mortensen, whom I used to idolise when he "guested" for Ashington and I was a ball-boy on the little north-eastern ground, cracked in three goals, Stan Pearson got another, and for good measure I used a Stanley Matthews centre to head my first goal for England.'
Jackie Milburn, on his début in the 6-2 victory against Northern Ireland in October 1948 as told in his autobiography *Golden Goals*

'I'd joined the squad hoping at best to get a place on the subs' bench, but on the morning of the game the boss took me to one side and told me I'd be playing. It was a big match for Wales and a great stage on which to make my international début, not that I had any reason to feel lonely because on the night Don (Revie) fielded a quite unbelievable nine new caps. In addition there were five Liverpool players in the side and my full-back partner from Anfield, Joey Jones, was lining up for the opposition. The game itself turned out to be one of the Revie era's better England performances. I played at right-back but wore number four just to confuse them and we ran out 2-1 winners thanks to goals from Ray Kennedy and Peter Taylor. I was reasonably pleased with my own performance and felt that I had done enough to begin to establish myself at least as a squad member.'
Phil Neal, on his England début against Wales in March 1976

'We just didn't watch our opponents or talk tactics in those days like we do today. Walter Winterbottom had seen them wallop France 10-1 and said they were a good side. But this was Wembley, and England had Matthews and Mortensen. You didn't tell players like that how they should play the game. You just let 'em get on with it..
   The trouble was we had never seen a deep-lying centre-forward before and just did not know how to deal with him. Hidegkuti pulled Harry Johnston out of position and, when he was picked up, it meant greater freedom for others. They didn't need much space anyway, they were so good on the ball.
   They came at us and attacked, something teams did not do to England at Wembley. It was a shock, all right, to find ourselves running around on our home ground chasing after players we had never heard of.'
Billy Wright, on the home defeat at the hands of Hungary in November 1953

Left: Terry Butcher, an England stalwart throughout the 1980s, also played under national manager Bobby Robson while at Ipswich Town.

ON PLAYING FOR ENGLAND

'I liked Sir Alf as a manager. He was so loyal to his players that in the end it may have been his downfall. He protected them from every outside influence. And, of course, when the team was doing well no one could get at him. He won the World Cup in 1966 and could have won it in Mexico in 1970. He picked me and stood by me when people were saying that I was too one-footed to be a player at the highest international level.'
Emlyn Hughes, in his autobiography *Crazy Horse*

'With me in the side were my colleagues, partner Jackie Mordue and right half-back Frank Cuggy, the nearest thing to perpetual motion I ever saw. The "Sunderland triangle" it was called.

'It was good to have team-mates at your side. I was not in strange company, as so many of our young players are in their first international.

'It is the unaccustomed atmosphere that, I think, accounts for so many failures on a first appearance for England. The player is keyed up to such an extent that it is almost impossible for him to produce his normal game.

'That is why I consider that a youngster should be given more than one game before being discarded. If he is good enough for selection, he is good enough for a second chance.

'Well, the result was a tremendous surprise. Ireland beat England 2-1, her first victory over her great rivals.'
Charles Buchan, on his début in the 2-1 defeat away to Ireland in February 1913 as told in his autobiography *A Lifetime In Football*

Left: Considered by many as the best inside-forward of his time, Charles Buchan won just six England caps, scoring four goals.

Above: Emlyn Hughes, correctly labelled by his club manager Bill Shankly as a future England captain.